The Bad Editor

Collected Columns and Untold Tales of Bad Behavior

Peter Jones

Bad Cat Library

You never know what is enough unless
you know what is more than enough.

- Proverbs of Hell, William Blake

For Kimberly Trent

FABRICE,
YOUR MY HERO!

PETER JONES

Table of Contents

Collected Columns

Untold Tales of Bad Behavior

Introduction

This book was created for the irreverent entertainment of motorcycle enthusiasts, not for spite or to even scores. Also, as a reading of these stories of bad behavior will reveal, much of the bad behavior is mine.

No names are mentioned, no brands are identified, and no guessing is encouraged. I like trying to tell a good story, and it has chafed me to leave some of the funnest ones untold throughout my career. They were untold simply because in the confines of motorcycle publications there isn't room for tales that stray too far from the central mission: motorcycles. I've learned that enthusiasts primarily want to know about the stuff. What's the fastest bike? What's the nicest jacket, the best tank bag? Will this bike make me a superhero? Human-interest stories in motorcycle periodicals need to be kept to a secondary minimum.

I have always operated on the presumption that I'm a pretty good person. But by compressing a number of my errant activities into this collection, I've started to wonder about that. Every month we humans make mistakes and do stupid things. But by leaving those deeds dispersed within the morass of one's mostly proper behavior, one's belief in oneself as a good person is justified. So, don't do what I've done here and put a pile of your bad deeds into one book while omitting your good deeds.

This book also includes a collection of 30 previously published columns I wrote for various motorcycle magazines. The columns were edited for clarity and to alleviate confusion about the transition of motorcycles in the last two decades. (We didn't used to have electronic rider aids and such.) Stories written prior to my father's death that mention him have been edited to refer to him in the past tense to match today's unfortunate truth.

The tales in this book are all true, with the caveat that they're mostly from an inadequate memory. Also, any mention of illegal behavior is simply the result of that bad memory and for the purpose of editorial enhancement.

Please enjoy.

Buffalo, New York
March 18, 2021

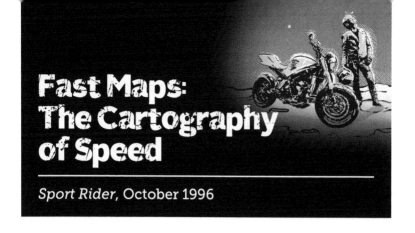

Fast Maps: The Cartography of Speed

Sport Rider, October 1996

Maps. Bird's eye drawings of roadways that help us get from here to there. A geographer friend tells me that maps are "graphic representations of relationships in space." Her definition probably isn't all that bad, considering that she is a geographer. But if that is the definition of a map, what help could one be to a road racer who spends all day on a road to nowhere? She has also taught me that there are maps that each of us use that are seldom discussed and little understood, yet religiously followed. These are referred to as mental maps.

Mental maps are maps that we draw in our mind's eye. They represent our personal view of the world. Their designs can range from actual representations of the world to unique constructs all their own — mental representations of relationships of space, emotions, intuitions and so on. Or for a racer, relationships of speed and time.

In 1994, my team (Team Pearls Racing) raced at Portland International Raceway (PIR) for the first time, offering me the opportunity to learn a lesson about mental maps and racing. Prior to practice, I walked the track with our riders, Darryl Saylor, Frank Wilson and Reuben Frankenfield, who were curious to see just where the thing went. They talked their way through each corner, discussing racing lines, pavement changes and details that might be worth remembering at speed. Civil engineers, of a peculiar sort, surveying and mapping the roadway.

The following day, after they each rode some laps, they drew a map of the track for discussion. Upon seeing their map, I was horrified at the confused "representation of relationships of space" they had drawn. I could not fathom how they could be so completely baffled as to the shape of the track's layout having now both walked and ridden its length. Yet they believed their drawing to be absolutely splendid. What happened next was even more disturbing.

A local racer, who had overheard their discussion about the track, offered them an official copy of a track map. They took the map, glanced at it for a moment, then tossed it aside and continued their discussion with their version. Were these guys boneheads or what?

It eventually dawned on me that I was wrong and that the map they had drawn was exactly correct. Whereas I would have created a map that represented relationships in space, they designed one that represented relationships in speed, time, thought and action. Not having ridden the track at race speed, I had not experienced it as they now had. For them, it no longer mattered where a turn was located, but rather what a turn meant.

Their version of the track depicted gigantic turns and very short straights. In reality, PIR consists of tight turns, third gear or lower, and two long straights. But for racers, straights are inconsequential. Straights are merely spaces between turns. Time between actions. Traveling in a straight line at 160 mph is boring and effortless. For racers, the turns are what need to be solved. All decisions, skilled actions and everything that separates the best from the rest are in the turns. The entry, the apex and the exit of turns are where the races are won and lost.

On their map, they identified where they sat up, braked, turned in, located the apexes, and where they began to pick the bike back up. Their map included precise measurements and details of each turn with the straights virtually ignored. Because of all the thought and action that it takes to attack turns correctly, racers picture turns hugely out of proportion to the straight sections of a track. The more technical the turn the larger it appears on a racer's map, regardless of its actual length. Their discussion included how the motorcycle was reacting and exactly what they were doing with the controls and when. For turns in close transition to each other, their mapping of the first turn was more of a picture of how to be in the right place to complete the second turn. They didn't care where the pavement went, but only where on it they wanted to be.

Race speed also taught them to relocate some of the apexes, that some pavement changes they had noted while walking didn't actually matter, and that ones they hadn't noticed did. On their map, distance was secondary to time, thought and action. It was a map of speed, not of space. As a team owner, you might think that this would be an interesting curiosity to me at best. But it is much more.

After a racer creates a map the racer discusses it with their crew chief to communicate what the map reveals about the bike's setup. Can a short-shift between two turns be solved with a gearing change? Can a suspension alteration settle the motorcycle through a particular transition? Does the suspension need to be altered for a gain in one place at a small loss in another? Data acquisition has helped this communication, but the rider's mental map will always be an important technical tool of feel. Just don't expect it to make sense on paper.

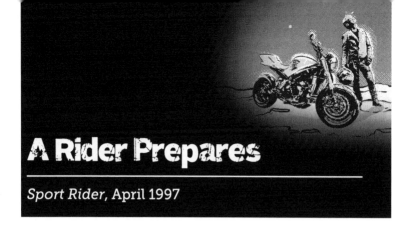

A Rider Prepares

Sport Rider, April 1997

Proof of the intense concentration and egoless nature of road racing presented itself to me as I approached turn one at Memphis Motorsports Park at about 145 mph. Nearing my braking marker, I sat up, reached out for the brake lever and began to awake from a trance. I felt like I was in that half-dream state of waking from an afternoon nap, when the fading thoughts of somnolent brain activity first mingle with conscious thoughts and the sounds of the outer world; normally the sounds of a passing car, children outdoors at play, a barking dog. My problem was that this time the sound invading my thoughts was the 12,000-rpm scream of a motorcycle engine between my legs.

As conscious thoughts flooded forward, I was astounded to find myself coming out of a trance and frightened that I had waited too long to brake. But a voice from within fought against this initial panic, telling me that my timing was correct and that braking would commence momentarily. Realizing this voice had somehow been guiding me around the track in my trance, and also because the timing seemed right, I gave in to its instructions.

After successfully entering turn one in this state, I relaxed and attempted to hold myself in this waking, half-conscious state to see what I could learn from this voice for an entire lap. As I circled the track, I gave myself up to a feeling, intuition, unreflected memory and a timing that came to me from within. I didn't actually decide when to sit up, brake, turn in and accelerate, but rather I let the rhythm of the track, the bike and the engine tell me how to ride. I was truly at one with the motorcycle and the track.

I noticed that I was a much better rider in that semiconscious state than when fully awake. I had moved my braking markers deeper into every corner while I had been in the trance. And when I had previously been fully awake and aware during practice sessions, my ego held me back from riding as well as I could.

That evening, as I contemplated what had happened on the track, a sudden rush of realization brought me back to a very similar experience from years earlier, back to when I was the Marquis de Sade.

I was a drama major during my first couple of years in college, and after eight frustrating weeks of rehearsing a scene from the play Marat/Sade, I found myself in front of an audience. When I then spoke Sade's words for the first time in front of an audience, his thoughts, feelings and intentions became mine. But I hadn't realized that I had fallen into a semitrance while performing until the scene was over and I came back to full consciousness in an extreme mental high, consumed by exhaustion.

That acting experience had shown me that it is the stepping outside of the ego and into a trance of intense concentration that is the true addiction of acting. Now the racetrack had taught me that might also be the true addiction of racing. Speed is a thrill on the street, but on the racetrack it is inconsequential. Regardless of the power of the motorcycle, if a rider is not running away from everyone else in a race, the only feeling of speed that he has is that he is going way too slow.

The real "thrill" of racing is the opportunity to step into another world; a euphoric, altered state of egoless thought that has no equal. This is the cause of the actor's and racer's "rush" and why we're so high after performing or competing. Adrenaline is not the cause.

I remained quiet about my semiconscious racing experience, fearing that fellow road racers might be a bit disturbed at the thought of competing against someone who is, in a way, asleep at the bars. But a few years prior to this experience, I had read that Formula One driver Ayrton Senna confessed that he would often fall into a trance during races. Unfortunately, all comparisons between myself and the late multi-time world champion Ayrton Senna end right there.

Thinking further about these experiences revealed to me more similarities between racing and acting: the superstitions, the odd loneliness, the pressure to perform, the escape to another world. The actor and racer give themselves up to a singular mission that is detached from all distractions. For a seasoned crew, when they see that their rider has put on his "race face," they know that it's time to leave him alone to prepare. This can be witnessed through how professional racers are with their bikes on the grid with their crew round them, and there is no chatting.

Because of the many distractions of professional racing, though, it's often difficult for a rider to mentally prepare prior to the warm-up lap. For that reason, the warm-up lap can be as much for adjusting a rider's head as it is for a last feel of the bike and look at the track. Rolling out from the grid, a rider isn't simply checking out the external conditions. He's also riding away from the world he shares with his team, his friends and his family, and into the private world of the racer.

Although racing is a team sport in many ways, for riders it's also very personal. For riders it feeds a selfish, all-consuming hunger. It's an addiction to an altered state of mind. Riders know that the only people who can truly understand this are those other addicts out there on the track with them, seeing a world transformed through each of their own internal and private transformations. The quote that sums this up best has been attributed to many racers, both real and fictional, but maybe that's because many actually have said it, each with their own self-discovered heartfelt originality: "To race is to live. All the rest is just waiting."

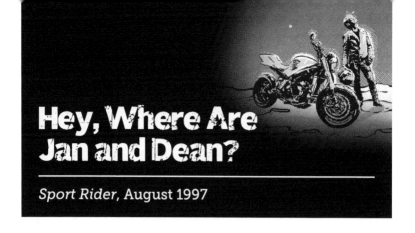

Hey, Where Are Jan and Dean?

Sport Rider, **August 1997**

The L.A. basin has more than 14.5 million inhabitants. Now that I live there, I feel as though humanity is crawling all over me. It's not that L.A. is a big city — it's just that the size of the bigness is so overwhelmingly huge. Airlines actually offer service on full-size passenger jets to take you from one side of this megalopolis to the other. Well, almost all the way. On the east side you'll still have to drive another 20 miles to reach the far edge.

To get a scale of this place, grab a map of the United States, cut out Chicago, and glue it into the space between Washington, D.C. and Baltimore. Your newly created city of Chiwaba pretty well approximates the size and population density of the greater Los Angeles metropolitan area.

But little can approximate the creativity of L.A. crime. Shortly after I arrived here, two bank robbers wearing body armor strolled down a street in North Hollywood shooting at everything that moved with their automatic rifles. As a result, the police may soon carry automatic rifles, too. This makes me feel especially safe considering the recent L.A. shooting between two motorists that was instigated by a stare and resulted in a death. They were both police officers in plain clothes.

As you now know, I am not from Southern California. I'm from Central New York. State, that is, not city. But somehow, after only eight weeks out here, the image of snow-covered dairy cows seems farther away than the 2800 miles it actually is. The image of an empty, grassy field seems even further away. Yet, there's something else they don't have any of out here, which to me is the most unsettling. Water. I'm beginning to suspect that L.A. might be in a desert.

I do like people, but there are two things that I'd prefer not sharing with everybody: my toothbrush and my lane on the highway. Every overly exaggerated, outlandishsounding, bad thing you've ever heard about L.A. traffic is absolutely true. Every road in this basin is constantly filled with traffic. Even on Sunday mornings. Where they are going, I do not know. Why they don't stay home and spend time with their families, I do not know. I do know that none of them are leaving, because the traffic never improves. They're all just driving around in circles. But I guess if you think about it, that's all any of us ever do.

In L.A., you have to fight your way through traffic on the city streets and on the freeways. The streets aren't as bad, because usually when splitting lanes on them it's between cars stopped at traffic lights. I have to admit that it does feel like cheating; cutting past everyone to the front row at every light. If the drivers don't like it, it really doesn't matter because you're gone as soon as the light changes. Gone to the next intersection to split lanes to the front. Always first in line. Cheating or not, I do it with guiltless joy. The rules are simple: If you want to be first in line, get a motorcycle.

There are risks though. The drivers in this place are worse than in any other city I've ever visited. In New York City, plenty of people do not know how to drive, but it's not a problem because they don't own cars. In L.A. everybody drives, every day, everywhere. I have to assume that they're doing it under the threat of death, because it certainly isn't being done with any joy.

At least one local radio station has traffic reports every six minutes. After listening to it for an hour, I was struck by the high number of accidents. And the station doesn't just report them as sites to avoid; they prefer to tell you the specifics of each calamity. "Multiple-car, fatality and personal injury accident in the number five lane with vehicles over the bank. It should be cleared in 20 minutes." It's amazing how quickly you can go from having a life to being a minor traffic inconvenience for others. Sort of like the herd leaving the weak behind. "Hey, too bad about that death and injury stuff, but we've got places to go."

It's also weird to see a car pulled over on the freeway by an officer of the law. With traffic moving bumper to bumper at either 80 mph or 5 mph (rarely at any speed in between), I am absolutely baffled in trying to figure out just what it is that one needs to do to get pulled over. Ram a police car? Shoot at other drivers? Have a leg protruding from your trunk?

Riding a motorcycle out here is also a remarkable experience in extremes. The population ends abruptly and totally at the foot of the San Gabriel Mountains, where some of the best sport-bike-riding roads in the entire country begin. These roads have no houses, no farms, no cattle crossings and barely any intersections or traffic. Yes, shockingly no traffic. Roads that consist of little other than curves. Lots and lots of curves. Roads of respite. Roads that can take you far, far away.

Potato Planters War in Vegas

Sport Rider, October 1997

Recently I attended the final round of the 1997 Supercross Series, held in Las Vegas, NV. I'd always wanted to see what the excitement over those hopping bikes is all about. Also, since it was a race event in a city famous for gambling, I figured it would be the next best thing to going to Monaco for the Formula One Grand Prix. Or, maybe not.

Prior to this, my only experiences of mixing bikes with dirt were attending a regional motocross event in the days when Bultacos were competitive, and taking part in a Tug Hill Plateau Poker Run on a 501 Moto Morini Camel — when Moto Morinis simply were. At the later event, my day featured getting completely covered in filth and laughed at by the other competitors for having worn a leather motorcycle jacket. What did I know? I thought we were going to ride on the dirt, not in it. I went with Joey Maier who was on a 125cc something or other. Again, what did I know? He toasted me in the woods. Bless whoever told me, "When in doubt, gas it." When we got to the gravel roads, I screamed by him at 70-plus mph. Compared to going through the woods at 15 mph, it seemed quite safe. Gas it. That's all I knew.

Two-thirds of the way to Vegas from Los Angeles I stopped in

Baker, CA, home of the world's largest thermometer. It is also home of some of the world's largest temperatures, which I'm guessing is the point of the thermometer's Colossus of Baker size.

Baker marks the southern approach to Death Valley, a valley that for my money is one of the most interesting godforsaken hellholes in America. There are not a lot of places where you can plant yourself down at 282 feet below sea level without your head imploding. Just don't be like the Germans and go there in the summer; you'll burn your wenig butt.

Finally, after about four hours of baked-brown emptiness, the promised land came into view as I rounded a bend with 15 miles to go. Being from Northeastern America, I am far too much of a wide-eyed innocent when confronting the sparkle of Las Vegas. There in front of me stood the Great Pyramid of Giza, New York City, a 14th-century castle and numerous other bizarre interpretations of transplanted histories and locations. In short, Las Vegas is a no-holds-barred exploitation of world cultures; it's a city where nothing is sacred and nothing is real. It is a paradise of bad taste where the guiding rule is: If too much is great, then far, far too much is even better. It's where obvious takes the place of opulence and mind-numbing fills in for nuance.

My favorite mockery of human civilization in Vegas is the Great Pyramid of Giza casino thing. As you would expect, in front of it sits the famous sphinx. But this sphinx is complete, as the original might have looked before Napoleon used his artillery to give the original one a quick nose job. Considered from the point of view of its historic context, there is a bit of weirdness to making a casino/hotel out of an ancient gravesite. One might wonder when the day will arrive for the Eastern Orthodox casino, graced with onion domes, or other such cultural misappropriations.

Finally arriving in Vegas, I was looking forward to getting out of the 105-degree heat and into the enclosed, air-conditioned Sam Boyd Stadium to see those jumping bikes. Or so I thought. It turned out that Sam is none of the above, though still quite adequate of a venue for the event. And while the desert is hell during the day, it is beautiful at dusk; the giant Nevada night sky provided a very nice roof.

Once seated on my portion of bench, I soon realized that I was in a sea of nearly 34,000 pubescent boys experiencing the joy and wonder of hormonal imbalance. In every direction pimples were being mauled and tortured. I felt old and out of place, and I have to admit that I kind of wished I had a zit or two of my own so that I could have contributed to the event's ambiance. When in Rome...or Vegas.

The event was awesome. Supercross rules! The first time seeing these guys do a cross-up over the triples is a scream. I can't tell you what I involuntarily said out loud. Seeing Kevin Windham click his heels together over his handlebars while flying 30 feet off the ground is a total gas.

As luck would have it, I chose to attend an event of historic proportions. Not only on this night was the 1997, 250 Supercross Championship decided and won by Jeff Emig on a Kawasaki, but this event also marked the first time in the history of dirt that a four-stroke machine won a Supercross. Doug Henry took the new Yamaha YZM 400F to a runaway victory over the field of screaming two-strokes.

The four-stroke bikes have remarkably changed the sound of Supercross events. After years of only two-stroke sopranos, the four-stroke baritones have arrived. Henry's bike seemed to produce a guttural grunt that's lower and wetter than any thumper I've heard before. Its sound is somewhere between Darth Vader doing a Bronx cheer and Hercules farting.

Great race, wacky town.

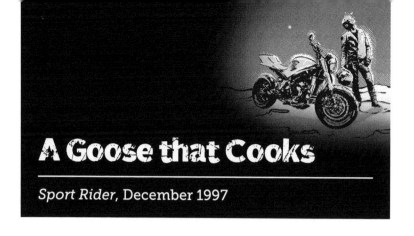

A Goose that Cooks

Sport Rider, December 1997

This job has affected my brain. Literally. Being an editor has caused weird physiological changes in the electro-neuro-synapses things that buzz around in the moldy, cheeseball that's inside my head. It has been a mind-altering experience. I'm not sure I know who I am.

Although I've spent much of the last seven years at the racetrack, I haven't actually been on one since 1993 so my high-speed instincts and cornering butt meter had gotten far out of calibration. That is one of the problems with managing a racing team. You no longer get to do all of those things that interested you in the sport in the first place, the main one being racing.

I am experiencing this mental metamorphosis because this job requires me to ride motorcycles as fast as I comfortably can. I now regularly find myself on racetracks, riding on that narrow line between "control" and "scared to death." Well, I never actually ride on that line but instead weave wildly back and forth across it: terror, comfort, terror, comfort, terror.... Sort of like an emotionally disturbed cat trying to determine just exactly how hot that stove really is.

But my return to the racetrack hasn't completely been a fool's paradise. My years of working with racers ensured maintenance of a reasonable technical knowledge of high-performance riding, and by my eighth lap of Willow Springs I was once again dragging my knees through the turns. Additionally, to research an upcoming article, I participated in a Penguin Roadracing School in Loudon, NH. While teaching me about the school, they also helped me chip a few layers of rust off my mental riding tools.

So anyway, this Russian woman and I were in Connecticut driving (in a car) along the Merritt Parkway, which is one of those old-world interstates built by civil engineers who valued beauty over safety. It has narrow shoulders, trees close to the lanes, fun turns and a narrow, bushy median.

Whipping along the left lane of this thing we came upon an animal running on the narrow shoulder next to the median. I immediately realized that the animal was running with the traffic and staying in its lane — so to speak. It being small, our closing speed was fast, and I soon saw that the animal was a goose. A goose in full gallop.

A goose in a road is not in itself a peculiar sight, but a goose that is in a full-out sprint is a bit strange to see. Its little webbed feet were kicking as fast as they could, propelling the chubby bird down the edge of road, with its butt in a high-speed sashay. Running with such intensity, the goose must have known where it was going and also that it was possibly going to be late. But for us, to where or why it was running will remain one of life's many mysteries.

Being a motorcyclist, I'd learned to look down the road and to write worst-case scenarios for riding's continuously changing contingencies. Writing such scenarios provides the tools to anticipate and react as quickly as possible to situations before they occur. This process has saved my skinny butt any number of times, allowing me to avoid injury and pain. Crashing hurts, and although you might not have noticed, I have found plenty of ways to harm myself.

Normally, I would have written a scenario of the possibilities the goose presented and been done with it. In this case, with all the traffic around us, the options of avoiding the bird if it turned to the right were closed. I admit that I was prepared to run over the cute little thing rather than kill myself, but because of the recent sharpening of my racing instincts, I did not write a scenario of doom. I wrote many scenarios of doom.

"The goose suddenly darts into the lane in front of us. Unable to swerve or brake because of the cars to our right and rear, we slam into the giant bird with the left corner of the bumper, taking it to the ground violently. I hold the steering wheel tightly as the right front tire...

"The goose turns to the right. Seeing our car at the last instant, it tries to take flight but we slam into it with the center of the bumper, sending it tumbling across the hood with its feathers flying...

"Just as we reach the goose, it turns right and leaps into the air. In an effort to avoid death, it tries to take flight, which results in it suffering a glancing blow off the corner of the bumper. As it tumbles into the windshield...

"Passing the bird startles it, causing it to suddenly turn right and run into the side of the car. I feel a gentle bump against the door and look in the rearview mirror to see...."

Enough already!! I killed the poor damn bird at least four times. In my head it just kept coming back at us like a Terminatoresque creature that just wouldn't stay dead.

This experience reminded me how riding is a mental game and showed me that my mental tools had been dulled through years of nonuse. It demonstrated that we can't fake mental habits and we can't fake knowledge. To increase our skills, we have to increase the intensity of the experience. In short, skill is a knife that is sharpened through use and dulled in storage. And as everyone knows, a dull knife is more dangerous than a sharp one.

As we drove off beyond the galloping goose, I watched it in my mirror the same as we first saw him — running his little ass off and sharpening his highway skills.

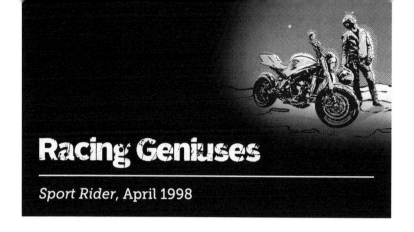

Racing Geniuses

Sport Rider, April 1998

Having recently participated in two riding schools — Freddie Spencer's High Performance Riding School in Las Vegas and the Penguin Roadracing School at Loudon — got me thinking about when I first went roadracing. It reminded me of the work it took to learn how to ride well.

Street-riding friend Tim Taylor and I both started racing about nine years ago. We decided to take up endurance racing and saw that the WERA National Endurance Series promised the virtue of maximum track time. It also had the vice of being, as most others would have likely noticed from its name, a national racing series. The implications of it being a national series were lost on me, so we packed a lunch and off we went.

We first had to bluff our way through the annoying requirements of a racing school and two race weekends in order to qualify to ride in the series. I thought those requirements were a silly nuisance and couldn't understand why they didn't just let us get out there and set some track records. What did those idiots possibly know about racing that I hadn't learned as a spectator? I'd show them.

Quickly in our first year of racing, Tim and I both broke our bones and had to sit out the second half of the season. Our first full-length endurance race was the following spring at Roebling Road Raceway in Georgia. It was a six-hour race and it was raining walls of water. Roebling is tight and twisty from turn one all the way back around to the front straight, allowing for really only one racing line in the wet. On each lap, riders would pack up behind me until we reached the front straight, then blast by leaving me in a blinding spray of water. Our scorer, Phil Arnold, told me afterward that it looked as if I was a giant cork plugging the flow of the field of bikes, until I exited onto the front straight allowing the bottled-up fleet to erupt past me. I didn't much appreciate what he was implying about my riding talents.

The race was stopped hours early because the puddles had become lakes and the lakes had become rivers. After the race, we checked the leaderboard and saw that we had finished around 40th!? I was shocked. Never in my life had I ridden so hard and fast in the rain. Well, except of course for the only other time that I had raced in the rain. I had crashed that first time. But this time I hadn't crashed, yet I began to suspect that this racing thing wasn't going to be as easy as I had thought. Although I still figured we'd win once we got to a dry track.

The next national was at Talladega Gran Prix Raceway in Alabama. The track is also known as "Little Talladega" because when most people hear Talladega they tend to think of the NASCAR track, which is a superspeedway. During practice we timed ourselves and our competition, discovering that while our lap times were around 1:12, most of theirs were at about 1:06. This was not good but we weren't embarrassed because we knew that their bikes were faster than ours. They were all riding

Honda Hurricanes while we were on a Suzuki Katana, which was a tad piggly on a racetrack. We were at a disadvantage that wasn't our fault.

Realizing that weekend that we couldn't complete six-hour races with only the two of us riding, particularly in a dry race, we looked for a local rider who might be interested in getting some free track time. A guy from Tennessee, by the name of Tray Batey, agreed to try out our bike.

Batey did a few laps during practice to see if we should make any changes to our bike's setup. On his first lap he did a 1:06. On his second lap he did a 1:04. Tim and I, standing next to each other at the pit wall with our stopwatch, looked at each other in stunned stupefaction. The true reason for the slowness of our lap times had been revealed to us. Almost simultaneously we each mouthed the words, "It's not the motorcycle." Batey had quickly taught us the most valuable lesson of our, up-to-then, short racing careers: Speed comes from within a rider, and fast guys are fast no matter what they ride. In a way, motorcycles are a bit like horses; they're only as good as the rider. Our bike was terrible. Now we knew from where the terrible was coming.

It wasn't really until months later, at the WERA National Endurance event at Indianapolis Motorsports Park, that I can claim to have become anything near what a true racer is. We had by then survived the 24 Hours of Nelson Ledges — which is a brutal experience that changes you for the better or the worse. We actually changed for the better.

By the time we reached the race at Indy we'd been through eight races, the shortest of which were six-hour events, and our bike was refreshed, overbored and rebuilt. Up to that point, my participation in the races had consisted of riding around the tracks alone, while nearly every other bike passed me. But in this race I kept running into traffic. As soon as I had fought my way by one rider I'd be trying to find my way around another. I thought it was really weird that there were suddenly dozens and dozens more bikes on the track than ever before, and so many of them were actually going slower than me. What had happened?

Soon I found myself trying to pass a racer who I was used to being lapped by repeatedly at every other event. As I closed in on him I thought at first that I can't pass him because he's faster than me. And then I passed him. It wasn't until then that I realized what had happened. I had finally made the leap from being traffic to being a rider who passes traffic. I had finally learned how to ride.

In our rush to go endurance racing, we had sort of forgotten to first learn how to race. For a racer to improve his craft he has to stick his hands into the fire to experience everything personally. Track time is why a racer is at the track, and nothing makes a racer faster than track time. It's a win-win proposition.

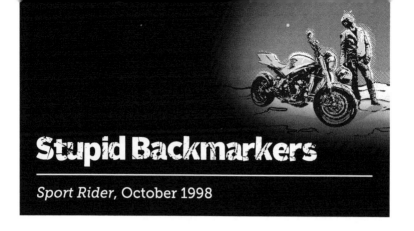

Stupid Backmarkers

Sport Rider, October 1998

Watching a road race recently, I was reminded of the insensitivity that some announcers and some factory riders have for "backmarkers." Much too often, backmarkers are spoken of as if they're untalented buffoons and senseless hazards to the real racers up front. I say it just ain't so. Well, for 90 percent of them anyway.

In the States, we witness the lapping of these "idiots" primarily in professional Superbike races, and there's good reason for that. The grid at any national AMA Superbike race consists of three sets of riders who reveal themselves after about the fourth lap of a race, which is how much time it takes for the speed differentials of these three sets to separate themselves into three tidy bundles. The starting grid is just an illusion that makes the riders look as though they are all in the same race. Their hearts are, but their motorcycles are not.

The first set of motorcycles on the grid consists of about a dozen factory riders who are paid professionals at the top of their form, racing on the best machinery available. No surprise there. The second set is made up of a few privateers who have spent their family's fortunes to build a Superbike that has a chance in hell of ever finishing better than 10th. It's a little like any State Lottery, except all it takes is $40,000 to buy the dream instead of a dollar.

The third, and largest, set of riders on the professional Superbike grid is on 750 Supersport bikes; aka Suzuki GSX-R750s. Regularly, a number of these riders will have finished in the top 10 in the Supersport race earlier in the weekend, and they are now again riding those same non-Superbikes with the hope of bringing home a few extra dollars. They know that by finishing 15th they'll win more than they could for finishing fourth in the non-purse-paying Supersport race. They are allowed to be in the Superbike race because without these riders there would only be a grid of about 14 motorcycles.

During the Superbike races, the riders on the Supersport bikes sometimes have the more interesting messages on their pit boards. Rather than the crew telling their rider his position in the race and the seconds back to the next rider, the crews sometime post the dollar amount the rider's current position pays, and the time distance forward to the next bigger payout. For example, a rider's pit board might read, "900-3-1100," which means he's three seconds behind a position that pays an extra 200 smackers. Money is an effective motivator. Go, baby!

More than anything else, backmarkers are in a real race for real money. They are all going as fast as they can, and it's not their responsibility to get out of the way of the factory riders. If it were, racebikes would have mirrors. They don't. Racers know that it is the responsibility of the ones passing to safely overtake, and it is the responsibility of riders being passed to basically ignore what is happening behind them. Trying to get out of the way is one of the most dangerous things a rider can do. On the other hand, when a rider sees a frontrunner challenging him for a track position, he is expected to concede the line without a fight. Purposely hindering the progress of motorcycles that are lapping a rider is not racing.

Because of the differences in speed and the encouragement by some announcers, some spectators have been getting lulled into believing that even they could ride as fast as those ridiculously slow backmarkers. In reality, that would be like believing you could outplay the guy on the end of the bench of any NBA team.

Honda Canada rider Frank Wilson was a competent Supersport bike-riding backmarker in the 1996 Superbike series. Also that year he took part in a track day at the Shannonville, Ontario, racing facility, which was open to street riders, too. Frank's street-riding friends knew all about his racing success (1995 Canadian Heavyweight Superstock National Champion, first privateer and 12th overall in the 1996 Daytona 200), but they remembered him only as the squid they used to ride with. So they made a bet that Wilson couldn't lap all of them within 10 laps.

They agreed to use the morning session on the track for practice so that the street guys would have time to learn their way around before the impromptu race. During this practice Wilson showed them his stuff, and by lunchtime all of his nonracer friends had begged out of the bet. For each one of them their concept of their riding ability had been severely shattered.

The point is, privateers and guys on Supersport bikes know how to ride, and it's primarily their equipment that makes them look so pathetically slow compared to the factory guys. To look at it from the backmarkers' point of view, the guys lapping them are just as much of an annoyance to them as these backmarkers are to those frontrunners. Giving up the line to the Superbike race leader at times gives an advantage to the Superstock rider behind them fighting for position.

Not only some announcers, but also some factory riders complain about backmarkers. The thing is, without them the show is lacking. The AMA needs them to fill out the grid, maybe showing that there is some bigger issue that needs to be addressed. Lappers, like turns, bumps and curbing, are a fact of racing. Anthony Gobert is one of the few Superbike riders who has given them their due. To ensure we all give backmarkers a little more, maybe we should start referring to the factory guys as "frontmarkers," senseless hazards to racers being lapped.

A Firm Resolve

Sport Rider, August 1998

Because I like to tell all, it's no secret after the previous issue of Sport Rider that I crashed a Kawasaki ZX-6R at the bike's introduction to the world press in Spain. Falling at 43 years old, in a foreign country, gave me cause to reflect on my long history of unplanned visits to the pavement. It got me to wondering whether I've chosen the right profession.

The first time I fell off of two wheels was the first time I ever rode a bicycle by myself, as is likely the same with most people. Everything had started out just fine in a straight line, but when I came to the turn at the end of our street I got a little confused and promptly fell over. Everything that I tried to do to steer the bike caused it to react the wrong way. Everything I did to correct everything I'd been doing wrong just made it all worse. At the time I didn't know anything about that counter-steering stuff, and I hadn't yet developed an intuition of feel.

I got it mostly right for a while after that, until my next crash of consequence, which I attribute to panic. I hadn't been paying attention to what was behind me, and when I went to move to the left it was into the path of a car coming up from behind me. So, while still looking rearward, l quickly swerved back to the right and rear-ended a parked car. I veered from the path of a moving car into the path of one that wasn't moving. I remember being confused about the violence as I tumbled across the car's trunk and into its back window, not yet knowing what I had hit.

My two worst falls on the highway both occurred in Pennsylvania, where my family spent its summers. There is a type of back road that is peculiar to Pennsylvania in how they are little more than paved Indian trails. It's as if the state just made one quick pass through the woods with a bulldozer and a paver and they were done with it. Who needs all that expensive heavy machinery anyway? Oh yeah, and then some guy came by later and painted yellow stripes down the middle, which never made a lot of sense to me because the roads are barely more than the width of a car. Additionally, by some unexplained bizarre phenomenon, the intersections of these roads are usually located on steep, blind, off-camber curves.

Back to my crashes. The first of these two falls was caused by "casing out," so to speak. I was making a tight right turn at one of those off-camber intersections, and the bike's pedal dug in lifting the rear wheel from the ground. Wearing shorts, my bare right knee planted into the pavement, picking up loose gravel. It hurt a lot. I still have the scars to prove it. I never again made a turn with the inside pedal at the bottom of its stroke.

I honestly can't take full credit for initiating my worst bicycle crash of all. Really. I didn't know it at the time but the bike that I had borrowed had a bent frame and the faster it was ridden, the worse it handled. At speed it weaved. Uncontrollably. Since I had just borrowed it, I didn't yet know that.

Riding with a few friends, we came to the descent of a long hill and as I gained speed the bike started weaving worse and worse. Since this was my first experience with such a thing, it caused me little concern and I continued to pedal as fast as possible. The weaving suddenly caused the bike to whip back and forth uncontrollably in a tank slapper that finally came to an end when the rear of the bike shot past me and I was spun around and thrown to the ground. I landed on my left knee this time, tearing a hole in my jeans and taking a giant, square chunk of meat out of my knee. That chunk is still missing.

I hobbled about a half-mile to the nearest house to call for help. Lying there on the porch of this kind stranger's home waiting for help to arrive, I remember that I was thinking about life, about pain and suffering, and about my history of crashes. I was becoming tired of getting injured. Realizing that the common factor in each of these falls and crashes was that they all happened while riding a bicycle, I resolved then and there to never ever ride a motorcycle. I figured that crashing something as fast as one of those things must hurt really badly, so there was no way that anybody was going to get me to do something that stupid.

Life decisions made while lying on your back with a bleeding knee are not to be followed through on. But I admit, it's often only by appearance that I'm unmoved by my traumatic experiences. I've by now fallen from motorcycles as many or more times as I've fallen from bicycles. And although I still hate pain, I have a passion for riding that is at least as powerful as my instincts of self-preservation. Risks and contradictions, that's life. I ride motorcycles. That's my life.

Plus, I really like wearing the cool leather outfits.

Everything is Something

Sport Rider, June 1998

This past summer's World Superbike (WSB) event at Laguna Seca was the first time that I got to see the world's finest four-stroke aces compete in real life. During that weekend in Monterey I also saw, in person, one of the guys who shares the responsibility for first enticing me into becoming a biker. Until that weekend, I had half-never-known and half-forgotten his impact on me.

Up to that weekend I'd always solely blamed my getting the motorcycling disease on my high-school friend, Damon Dardaris. Damon was born a motorcycle nut. In our late teens he used to drive the guys we hung out with, and me, crazy with his incessant talk about bikes, bikes, bikes. We showed him patience by listening to his ridiculous tales about motorcycles but little did we know that he was infecting our fragile minds. The sickness would fester in our souls until many of us eventually started telling others ridiculous tales about bikes. Now I earn a living doing it. Ha.

As a teen, the walls of my bedroom were plastered with posters, mostly of nearly indecipherable psychedelia. A few of my posters, though, featured rebels of the day, each of whom happened to be sitting on a motorcycle. They were Peter Fonda in a still from the film *The Wild Angels*, Steve McQueen on the Triumph he rode in

The Great Escape, and Dennis Hopper in his final gesture at the end of the film *Easy Rider*. As a teen, though, my solidarity with these antiheroes was one only of civil disobedience, not motorcycling. As a troubled youth I found it reassuring to know that there were troubled adults to look up to.

When the film *Easy Rider* was released in 1969 my father took me to see it. As you most likely know, it is a film about two ex-stunt riders, Billy and Wyatt, looking for America. I think that my father was hoping that the film might offer him and me a means to communicate with each other during those tense times.

Easy Rider enthralled me. It was the first film I had seen that depicted the counterculture from the point of view of the counterculture. And it did it with a bit of intelligence. Both culture and counterculture came off looking equally unpromising. The film captured the confusion, hatred and fear in the streets of those times, and smartly responded without any answers.

But. At the time, the fact that they were on motorcycles seemed to me only a symbolic way to communicate that they were rebels. I saw their motorcycles as just dramatic devices. But it didn't take long until I had that iconic poster of Hopper, from the film's final scene, displaying the international gesture of brotherly love and goodwill. It was just the sort of role model I had longed for.

In '73, on the way home to Syracuse from a visit to Martha's Vineyard, my friend Damon insisted that we take a 100-mile side trip to Boston to see a motorcycle. The bike was an 810-kitted, Dunstall Honda CB750. At the time, it was kind of neat looking to me but not much more than that.

A year later, Damon and I drove to California in my rusty 1969 AMC American. I was on my way to the San Francisco Art

Institute to study filmmaking. One of the silly points that I got out of *Easy Rider* was that film could be used as an art to inspire people to think about and to question ideas, just as this film helped a father and a son communicate. It inspired me to want to make movies. But somewhere inside me the motorcycle infection had also taken hold.

The deal between Damon and myself was that we would stop at the Yoshimura facility on our way to San Francisco. This time our meaningless bike-related side trip was a mere 600 miles out of our way. But I knew that visiting Yoshimura was a religious experience to him. So I was not about to get in the way, though I didn't even know what Yoshimura meant.

As bad luck would have it, Yoshimura had closed for the day just before our arrival and we were unable to go inside. Even so, Damon had found one of the exiting employees, who kindly chatted with him for about 15 minutes. As we left, I thought that the visit was a failure. But it soon became clear that for Damon it was a thrilling adventure fulfilled that would well up in him for days.

For various reasons, I was distracted from pursuing filmmaking, but within a couple of years from then I could no longer resist the attraction of motorcycles. And although my enthusiasms leaned toward the sportbike side of the motorcycling sphere, that is nothing more than a technical preference. To me, the culture of bikes includes all motorcycles.

Back to this past summer's WSB event at Laguna Seca. While there, I learned that Dennis Hopper was having an opening of his photography work that weekend at a local gallery in Carmel-by-the-Sea only a few miles away. The concept of a reception honoring my quintessential rebel biker dude, in coincidental concert with a race weekend, intrigued me. And even though Easy Rider might have been nothing more than a moment in Hopper's life, it was also a moment in my life and it had contributed to me being at Monterey that very weekend.

So, after final practice on Saturday we headed for the opening. I figured that all we'd get to do was see his pictures and eat some hoity-toity crackers, so I was a little stunned when we found Mr. Hopper there in the living flesh. Seeing him gave me pause to reflect, bringing a side of my life full circle. No one else from the race event was there and I doubted that he would be at the track the next day. Neither one of us was having thoughts of the other and neither cared. As I've learned many times, there are few who see the world in the same sparkly lights that illuminate mine.

The next day, between the two legs of the WSB races, Kent Kunitsugu and I were on the back of stunt rider Gary Rothwell's bike doing wheelies and stoppies the length of the front straight. I thought for a moment about a couple of wandering ex-stunt riders from long, long ago. I was reminded once again that a motorcycle is not just a motorcycle.

The Big Show: "The Art of the Motorcycle" at the Solomon R. Guggenheim Museum

Motorcyclist, October 1998

Writing an article about a display of 114 motorcycles in a museum should be a straightforward no-brainer, no? This is a motorcycle magazine, it's a motorcycle exhibit, and I'm a motorcycle journalist. So my job is obvious: just talk about the motorcycles. Well, it's not that simple.

The problem is, this isn't just a motorcycle exhibit. If it were, it would be at a history or motorcycle museum. And it would be attended by you and me: truant children and tourists looking for a bathroom. While touring the exhibit, since we've all been there before, we know the program: hang out, splay our plumes, ram our horns, sniff each other's butts, hoof the ground and snort repeatedly, "Nice bike." Motorcycle exhibits have always been little more than biker-bonding benefits. Bike exhibits were for us, and that's how we liked it thank you very much.

But this motorcycle exhibition isn't just for motorcyclists. It isn't at a history museum or a motor-vehicle museum. It's at an art museum, and it is not just any art museum. This exhibition is at one of the most globally respected museums of modern art: the internationally renowned, Frank Lloyd Wright-designed, Upper East Side-addressed, black-tie swank, holy house of 'isms, bastion of high-taste cultural purity, fortress of fine art, Solomon R. Guggenheim Museum. Whoa! Break out the clean T-shirts kids. This ain't no stinking bike exhibit, it's a cultural event of high culture.

As if that doesn't complicate things enough, the installation of *The Art of the Motorcycle* exhibition is in itself an artistic statement, designed by world-renowned architect Frank Gehry. The installation features polished steel covering the Guggenheim's spiraling inside skirt of the spiraling parapet that flows around and around for a quarter mile from the center of the rotunda floor to its terminus six floors above. This reflecting ribbon of floating steel creates the effect for visitors of being inside a giant valve spring gone mad. It's appropriately mechanical and dynamic.

So why motorcycles at the Guggenheim? What gives? Ever since Life magazine crucified motorcyclists in 1947 with what has been revealed as a staged image from Hollister, CA, featuring a beer-drinking biker parked amongst a sea of empty beer bottles, we motorcyclists (bikers) have been looked at as the lowest low of whatever has crawled out of the mire. And even at the opening of this exhibition, I overheard — I swear to God — a woman remarked that more "scooter trash" had shown up than she expected.

Scooter trash?! Them's fightin' words lady.

So how'd this bike show come to be? It was an inside job, that's how.

Director of the Guggenheim Museum Thomas Krens is a

motorcyclist. So Krens understands the motorcycle culture from our point of view; from the seat of a bike on the highway. Due to his career in the world of high-culture fine art, Krens had the inkling that a motorcycle exhibition could provide a unique vehicle for interpreting the evolution of 20th-century design and culture.

Adding to this, Krens happened to have a kindred motorcyclist on staff: fellow biker Ultan Guilfoyle who heads the Guggenheim's Film and Video Production Department and whose experiences include filming the TT races at the Isle of Man for the BBC. To assist in ensuring historical accuracy, motorcycle historian Charles Falco was brought on board. In real life, Falco is Director of the Laboratory for X-Ray Optics at the University of Arizona. He's also, of course, a biker and — although not quite a spring chicken — road races, too. He's easily the fastest Chair of Condensed Matter Physics on two wheels. These three, Krens, Guilfoyle and Falco, are the ones at whom fingers will be pointed when the inquisition begins.

The intent of this exhibition is to tell a story about the 20th century through the evolution of a product of mass consumption, a product whose life is, so far, a century long. But as the curators of the exhibition and the rest of us motorcyclists all know, motorcycles are much more than just products. Not only do bikes have mechanical and design aesthetics, largely governed by form follows function, they also possess powerful cultural and social meanings and elicit strong emotional responses. That's exactly why motorcycles were chosen for this exhibition rather than chairs or toasters.

All that said, it is surprising that other than a few sales brochures presented separately, the exhibition has nothing on display except motorcycles. For us bikers, that's great. What else matters? But if something about motorcycles and our culture is to be communicated to nonbikers, it would seem that the machines might need to be interpreted in some kind of historical, social or aesthetic context. Or with words.

There are, admittedly, words in the exhibition catalog: *The Art of the Motorcycle*, which is an exceptional publication that all motorcyclists should purchase — big, thick and colorful. Nearly every motorcycle in the exhibition is featured in the book in multiple blackand-white and color pictures with a short description. The book also includes eight essays about the history and culture of motorcycles, most of which are excellent. But the exhibition itself on the floors of the museum offers little in the way of interpretation.

Because of the (mostly negative) cultural history of motorcycles in America, it is impossible to look at bikes in the same way that we look at automobiles, or, really, any other products. Motorcycles carry with them a burdensome load of cultural baggage that overwhelms those two little contact patches where the tires meet the pavement. In the USA, people don't buy motorcycles because they're an inexpensive or practical means of transportation. Also, riders don't buy Harley-Davidsons because they have good resale value. People buy bikes because they're, well ... bikes, and because those people are bikers. Within our borders, motorcycles are enthusiast products with specific, unavoidable, powerful connotations about love, hate, sex, fear, death, life, danger and power. For motorcyclists, bikes are the very coolest self-defining objects that we possess. Bikes are the kinetic, dynamic, living icons of our religion.

So, for us motorcyclists, there is a certain amount of indecency in this exhibition: this tossing of our pearls before swine, this speaking of the names of our gods to the ears of the unenlightened. An exhibition of motorcycles, to the average museum patron, is somewhat like an exhibit of tribal culture from faraway or like an exhibit of a lost civilization from long ago. Or, maybe it's like the monkey cage at the zoo. There's just no grounding reference point for most museumgoers. All those glossy art magazines and years of art appreciation courses provide few tools for interpreting this exhibition.

In this leather-meets-linen, cross-cultural nexus, the tables are turned: We *hoi polloi* biker people — who would use the royal seal as a nutcracker — are here the sublimely cultured ones while the art-loving, Neiman Marcus-shopping, limo-riding, art-museum patrons are the uneducated, ignorant, heathen swine. We know bikes to our bones. We live bikes. We smell like bikes. We have fingers stained from bikes. What do those cultivated sophisticates know? They don't know the wind in the face, motoring on warm summer nights, the feel of leaning through a turn, the catharsis of hours in the saddle, twisty roads, musical exhaust notes, a week's riding in the rain, the power between our legs. Forget all of that. They don't know a Panhead from a bevel drive from a one-lunger. They don't even know where the clutch lever is located or what sequential shift pattern means.

All of that is what makes it easy to spot the bikers at this exhibition; not by how they look but by how they see. Motorcyclists have the tools, the passions, the training and the culture to know the importance of a particular casting, the aesthetics of a manufacturing process, the beauty and economics of a design. The bikers are the ones staring at bolt heads, tire treads, welds, folds and fasteners, at design solutions and mechanical efficiencies.

It's that word "art" in this exhibition's title that complicates matters. Guilfoyle explained that it is an exhibition of design, not art. But since it's an art museum, there are all sorts of mental baggage involved that colors expectations. Additionally, museum patrons know that they're in an art museum so they can be agreeable to looking at the bikes as works of art. It is what they know. Art museums are where people go to see art, and the Guggenheim is known for its collection of modern art. Much of that art is esoteric in its meanings and is difficult for the untrained viewer. Much of modern art looks like ugly crap to the "uneducated" because it is about art, not about the day-to-day human experience. Being duller than most, I didn't come to this conclusion cheaply. It took me half of my life and a bachelor's degree in fine arts, plus a year's work toward a master's, before I figured out how to be a philistine without guilt.

But motorcycles do not fit into the above description of art because they are everyday objects of the human experience and they are designed to serve a function. Motorcycles' meanings are in their use, not simply in their being about something else, as is often the case with paintings, sculpture and the fine arts. It could be said that what we have with this exhibition is an art museum owning up to the realities of modern culture and admitting (maybe inadvertently) that modern art might not be as relevant to defining the human experience as are the products we use, live with, consume and love.

There is nothing that occurred in the history of motorcycles in America that has the potential of this exhibition to sanctify motorcycles for the masses and, maybe more importantly, for the ruling class. The simple fact that this exhibition is at the Guggenheim has significant ramifications. And it is as if, due to this exhibition, motorcycles have passed through the Pearly Gates of cultural acceptance. George Barber, owner of the Barber Vintage Motorsports Museum that loaned the most motorcycles for this exhibition, told Falco that he believed this exhibition could change the history of motorcycling in America. Hollister 1947, Guggenheim 1998; maybe the bookends of motorcycling's 51-year-long fall from grace.

But wait, do we really want redemption?

If this exhibition does change the history of the motorcycle, it will probably affect us in the same way that Woodstock affected the counterculture of the 1960s, announcing its end and not its beginning. We could lose more than we gain. Like the 1960s counterculture after Woodstock, our subculture could become diffused into the inanity of the mainstream with all meaning washed away by everyone having a motorcycle in their garage. Consider that everyone already has a tattoo and black leather jacket. Before we know it, we'll be respectable. It's impossible to rebel if your chosen life style is the common commerce of department stores.

All that said, regarding this exhibition for you and me, screw the cultural crap, the pretense, the pomp, the question of art; screw the flashy installation and Uptown address, just screw all of the possible lofty intentions. What then have we got? The best damn collection of motorcycles ever in one place at one time, that's what. It is a collection that will impress any and every biker out there regardless of experience, knowledge or niche interest. It's a collection of nearly every bike that we all knew was important, together with all the important ones most of us had never heard of before. And it's all under good lighting!

It might be best if no one from the *New York Times* reads this, but the bottom line is that Krens, Guilfoyle and Falco are scooter trash just like us. As to whether or not this endeavor of theirs will actually make motorcycles acceptable to the talkthrough-closed-teeth crowd, only time will tell. Sure, the exhibition communicates that motorbikes are pretty and that our subculture is cute. But the real test is whether or not the members of the Guggenheim's Board of Trustees will now let us date their sisters and daughters.

The Art of the Motorcycle was open through September 20, 1998 at the Solomon R. Guggenheim Museum, 1071 Fifth Ave., New York, NY 10128. The exhibition was sponsored by BMW, the installation by Banana Republic. The show featured more than 100 motorcycles, from the very first Michaux-Perreaux steam-powered bike of 1868 to the 1999 MV Agusta F4. The Art of the Motorcycle was curated by Guggenheim Director Thomas Krens, with curatorial assistance by Charles Falco, Ultan Guilfoyle, with Matthew Drutt, Sarah Botts and Vanessa Rocco contributing to the catalogue.

Two publications were available in conjunction with the exhibition: a fully illustrated, 432-page exhibition catalog titled *The Art of the Motorcycle*, distributed through Henry N. Abrams and available in hardcover for $85.00 and in softcover for $45.00; and *Motorcycle Mania: The Biker Book*, published by Universe Publishing and available only in hardcover for $27.50 [At the original date of this article's publication.]

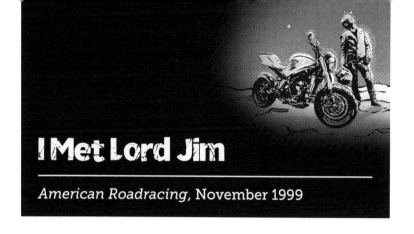

I Met Lord Jim

American Roadracing, November 1999

This is the first issue of *American Roadracing* created by its new owner and staff. I'm supposed to take this opportunity to blather on about all the great and wonderful plans we have, why we won't suck, and tell you how we're going to absolutely change the face of motorcycling. OK, there, I just did that. Now let's get on with something meaningful.

As you may have read in any number of motorcycling publications, racer Stewart Goddard was seriously injured while competing in the Aprilia Challenge Cup 2000 race at the Formula USA Pocono Cycle Jam on the last weekend in August [1999]. Stewart crashed after going off the track on the first lap of the race "while trying to avoid a downed rider who had fallen in front of him." That's how it was reported in most places, which is exactly how it should have been reported. Had I been any other human being in the world, there would be nothing in the above quoted sentence to redress. But I'm not any other human; I am that "other rider."

If you didn't already know, there's something about Stewart racing that is remarkable. He is paralyzed from the chest down, the result of a moped accident when he was a teenager. But he is a motorcycle enthusiast through and through, so even though his injuries are permanent he has never allowed them to get in the way of pursuing his dreams and goals. Wanting to ride a motorcycle again, through the gracious help of some friends, Stewart had a CBR900RR fitted with outriggers to hold the bike up whenever he came to a stop, and Stewart took to the streets.

After riding on the street for a while, Stewart developed a desire to go roadracing. And, again, through the help of others, he found himself on a 125 GP bike competing regularly at Willow Springs International Raceway. Despite Stewart's intimate knowledge of pain and suffering, he chose to go racing and he chose to do it with the full hunger of any racer. When the Aprilia Cup races were announced, Moto Liberty stepped up to provide him sponsorship for the season. That's how I first got the opportunity to meet him, at the RS250 press intro in Las Vegas, NV last January.

Stewart, more than anyone else I've ever met or heard about, is unassailable proof that a person involved in a high-risk sport could do so while knowing full well the risks involved. It could always be argued that racers who have never been seriously injured don't really and truly comprehend the dangers and possible consequences of the sport. But no one could say that about Stewart. He's been there. He knows exactly and intimately what a life-altering injury is all about. So I was interested in talking to Stewart about this because I'd been writing an extended story about risk and racing.

Stewart responded enthusiastically and openly about risk and why he was racing. I admit that I had been hesitant at first to enter into this discussion with him because, although risk might be a preoccupation of mine, it's not something with which active racers should bother themselves. Racers need to know the risks of racing, accept them, and then never give it another thought.

I was also hesitant to talk about risk with him because I didn't know how Stewart perceived himself. I mean, maybe he lived in denial and didn't know he was in a wheelchair. If so, I sure didn't want to be the one to reveal this to him. Stewart, though, sees life clearly and was eager to talk, which provided us with a quick intellectual bond.

And then the race at Pocono.

In one quick, violent smack to the ground, all of the study I'd put into understanding risk seemed suddenly meaningless. Being a racer had shown me risk firsthand. Falling and breaking my bones revealed, within my own flesh, the possibilities of personal injury. Various crashes showed me that there are plenty of things that can happen on a track that are out of a rider's control, despite racers believing that they are in control. But now I'd been shown that there was a major detail about risk that I'd never properly considered: The risk at which one racer puts another. Plus, this incident went beyond that with the added ironies of the badly injured rider being a friend, and being Stewart Goddard, of all people. That shouldn't mean anything special, but it's hard for it not to.

To other riders involved in incidents like this, countless times I've told them, "It happens. We all know the risks. Forget about it. No one is to blame." I thought I knew what I was talking about. This, though, was the first time that I'd found myself in the role of the "other rider." The view is a lot different from over here. Depression and guilt characterized my week following the incident.

I've had many ugly thoughts, such as considering the benefits of disappearing from this profession altogether, and worse. As a motorcycle journalist, I'm not allowed obscurity in this sport. My life in motorcycling is public. And off the track, in the day-to-day course of business, I have to face people from industry insiders to readers who know about this incident. If I were just a regional racer going home to a regular job, no one in my daily life would know anything about it. So hiding from the incident could offer a means of hiding from the guilt.

There aren't supposed to be parties to blame for racing incidents and riders aren't supposed to carry guilt with them, regardless of how tragic an accident turns out to be. As I've said, racers accept the risks. But I cannot pretend to be blind to the simple physical cause-and-effect relationship of this incident. My involvement is clear and undeniable. So there is guilt. And I now realize that a rider in my situation would always feel guilty, or he's not human. Initially, guilt is fine and normal. But finding a balance between a healthy measure of guilt and an obsession with blame can be very difficult.

Many friends called or wrote that week saying, "It happens. We all know the risks. Forget about it. No one is to blame." Those words seemed foolish and empty and, worse yet, they even increased my feelings of guilt. For these people to bother to concern themselves with my emotional state while Stewart is so badly injured felt unfair. My thoughts were that it was wrong to waste time consoling me; Stewart was the one who was injured. I resented being consoled. I didn't ask for it and I didn't want it. I just wanted people to leave me alone and let me feel bad. It was my guilt and it was my right to wallow in it.

In many ways, I got off easy because Stewart will recover about fully from the crash, although it is doubtful he will ever race again. There was a cost to this event. But in looking at the big picture, that can't be the consideration for anyone in my position. A person has to put tragedy behind them regardless of its severity, otherwise they can no longer live a normal life. But how does one do that? Those calls from friends were important, meaningful, and in the end they were greatly appreciated. When one is emotionally confused and feels no longer welcome to participate in the human experience, those reaching out to extend an invitation to return to the fold are indispensible.

"*Lord Jim*"? It's a book by Joseph Conrad that I read as a child. Oh, alright, I read the *Classic Comics* version. Anyway, in the book the title character destroys his life because of a guilt he can't go beyond. I now understand Jim's heart in this classic novel; his aching for a punishment that he feels that he deserves. So I tell myself, don't be like him. "It happens. We all know the risks. Forget about it. No one is to blame."

Life is a balancing act. Plates break. Go forward.

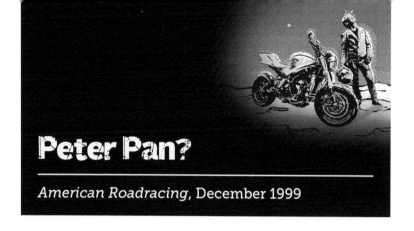

Peter Pan?

American Roadracing, December 1999

"**W**here the hell am I, and how'd I get here?" I remember thinking that same thought years ago, after waking up one spring morning when I was 20 years old. I was a little too young to have been a part of the '60s but a little too old to be untouched by them. I was just finding my stride in the early '70s, but the party had been shut down a few years earlier and no one quite knew what to do next. Being lost on your own is one thing, but being lost together with a generation is something else altogether.

Jump to the early '90s, and I was at some racing event having breakfast with a mechanic friend about 10 years my junior. I was doing my usual flirt with the waitress but it was going nowhere, not even on the low level of simply friendly attention that I was giving her. He was flirting too, and it was going everywhere. This, in itself, would have gone unnoticed by me had it not been yet another in a growing list of my failed flirts. I had lost my charm but I could not figure out where or when that had happened. So I asked him if he had any idea why I was becoming such a failure at flirting. He said that young women don't appreciate an old guy flirting with them.

Old guy!? Where? Who? What old guy?

About four years ago, I got a call from a prominent businessman and son of an ex-mayor of the city I was then working in as the director of the local history museum. He had called to ask if I'd please be an officer on the Board of Directors of the Chamber of Commerce. Specifically, the Vice President of Tourism and Promotion. I agreed to the appointment and soon found myself dragged into the process of approving bylaws for that city's soon-to-be-created Tourism Board and interviewing people for the position of Tourism Director. In a moment of fatigue, I remember looking out the window of my office at a ginkgo tree's branches waving in a cold fall wind and wondering to myself where that confused 20-year-old kid had wandered off to. Wondering to myself, "Where the hell am I, and how'd I get here?"

And now, again, I am wondering…. But, I'm not really lost. It's just the fatigue. Two magazine issues in six weeks can do that to a guy. But I still stopped to give it some thought.

A number of friends of mine who were into motorcycles some 20 years ago have, for one reason or another, sold or garaged their bikes for two decades. I didn't really get into bikes until my mid-20s, and I didn't go racing until my mid-30s. So I was just getting into the sport when these guys suddenly went off to make more humans and do other weird adulting stuff. Now, just as suddenly, they're all back riding again. And their sons or daughters are riding with them on their own motorcycles. Funny how that works. But what was up with that 20-year-long disappearing thing?

I seem to have missed a few things that were obvious to others. Some might offer that one of those things is growing up. I tried, it just didn't fit on me. Looking back at a few uncomfortable moments that occurred during the last 20 years, I now understand things a little better — such as the look I used to get from a friend's wife when I'd go over to ask if Johnny could come out and play. "No. He's busy raising a family. Go away."

For some reason, in all my years on this planet, the part about growing up and getting a career, and creating a family, and acting "right" never quite sunk in. I'm told that most guys don't go off racing motorcycles at 34 years of age. And most guys don't change careers four times in their life. Five. And that most guys don't... whatever. I've come to learn that it is exactly because of my never having understood these common expectations that I am in the motorcycle industry and in my present position. It's an industry run largely by people who have followed their hearts rather than some set of unwritten rules or a reasoned career plan.

Motorcycles are scary to many people, but maybe not because they're dangerous and not because they're noisy. Instead, maybe it's because they represent freedom, and freedom is often equated with irresponsibility. The party line says that good, respectable, responsible people don't have time for freedom — except maybe every now and then on weekends, after the lawn is mowed. But for a whole life? That ain't right.

In a perfect world, motorcycles should mean nothing. The meanings attributed to them culturally have been primarily placed there by nonmotorcyclists who have tried to explain why bikes aren't quite right. "Bikes" starts with a B and that rhymes with T, and that stands for trouble.

In the past, I've been uncomfortable with how those with preconceived notions of how a life should be lived have looked at me. But I'm over that now. Twenty-year-old waitresses will not again start appreciating my flirting, but that's OK. I really do know where I now am, who I now am, and how I got here, and there I have no shame and no regrets. Most importantly, I also know where that 20-year-old kid now lives — inside me.

Oh, and that freedom thing? It actually is a very big responsibility. I accept that.

Now, if I could only find some more time to ride...

Revenge of the CB350

American Roadracing, January 2000

started out as a car guy. Don't hate me. I had a few friends who rode bikes, raced bikes, loved bikes, but for some reason I loved cars. Sure, I had a minibike at one point and stole rides on scooters and anything else with two wheels that I could get my hands on. But as a child I lusted for a go-cart, not a motorbike.

So as I grew to the age where motoring lust turns its attentions toward actual street-going vehicles, my motoring dreams and aspirations were filled with sports cars, not sportbikes. But this might partially be because back then there wasn't such a thing as a sportbike. There were cafe racers, but if you wanted one you had to build it yourself or drive hundreds of miles to seek out obscure and unknown brands of bikes, like Ducati for instance.

I didn't buy a bike until I was in college in Tampa, FL, and not until cars had failed me. I had driven to Florida from my home state of New York in my sports car — a Fiat 124 Spider, specifically. But since that car was a Fiat, and since that car had lived in upstate New York for six years prior to it taking me to Florida, it had become less of a car and more of a rolling example of how quickly improperly protected carbon steel can transform itself back into its natural ferric iron state. Rust, that is. But as long as the top went up and down and the engine started, I was stylin'. I was James Bond on a budget.

Well, one day the engine didn't start and I was no longer stylin'. Rust wasn't the specific cause of death though. It was electrical fire. So since I was living in Florida, I decided to skip replacing the car and get myself a motorcycle. Back then, bikes cost much less than cars to buy, insure and operate. Plus, in Florida there weren't any stupid tests for riding them. A driver's license was a driver's license, period.

So I bought a repainted 175cc Kawasaki dual-purpose something or other. Yes, I confess, I don't remember what model of bike it was and I'm not sure I ever knew. It had two wheels and an engine, what else mattered? Apparently I am one of about 32 Americans in the history of motorcycling who actually bought a bike simply because it was an inexpensive means of transportation, not because it's cool to ride a motorcycle. I wasn't a motorcyclist, I was a commuter. Maybe I shouldn't have admitted this?

But the bike died a quick and puzzling death. It started its death by revving wildly, building up so much heat and rpms that I couldn't shut it off with the kill switch. It eventually revved out of control, and holding the kill button fully pressed did nothing to stop it. I had to put the bike into gear, hold the rear brake on, and dump the clutch. The bike stalled, but second gear came up missing. At the time, I didn't realize that the problem was caused by the carb — which was enclosed in the crankcase — leaking fuel that was then drawn into the engine causing it to scream out of control regardless of what I did with the throttle. Anyway, right there was born my hatred for two-strokes. I needed to get a four-stroke motorcycle always from then on. Well, except once more.

I soon after that found a Honda CB350 advertised on a bulletin board on campus. It said on the ad that the bike didn't run, $50. I went to look at it and it looked like a motorcycle. It was Florida-looking too, with the paint burned off the tank and the coloring on the gauges faded white. When I asked the owner why it didn't run, he told me that he was just out riding along one day and it stopped. That was good enough for me. "I'll take it!"

For me, this purchase was not just of a motorcycle, it was a means to immerse myself, for real, in the sport of motorcycling fully and with heart. I was much happier buying a broken bike than one that worked. Not just because of the attractiveness of that foolish economy, but because of how it forced me to understand the bike inside and out. Before I could ride it, I had to understand it and cure it.

I tore the engine down, discovering that the cam chain had jumped, mistiming the cam to the crank and putting the valves into the pistons. Since the art of cause/effect diagnosis of engine failure was still beyond my comprehension, I replaced the cam, the valves, the cam chain guides, and that's all. The chain seemed a little tight in spots but I figured it would get better. Or something. Obviously to any seasoned mechanic, the engine had stopped running because the cam chain had jumped so the valves were opening at the wrong time, which had a cause. Opening at the wrong time resulted in them being bent, but I didn't go to the root of determining why the chain had jumped. I thought it might have been because the guides were bad. It never dawned on me that it could have been the other way around. I was, of course, practicing bad medicine and it would eventually come back to bite me.

Anyway, I finished the rebuild and, to my astonishment, the

motorcycle actually started and stayed running after just a few kicks. And it sounded the way an engine is supposed to sound. Robust, not tinny. It was the sound of manliness and the open road. It was the sound of freedom. It was the sound of my future.

Just as I finished the rebuild, I went and graduated from college and had to head back north. I initially planned on shipping my stuff home and riding my bike to New York, and I told all of my friends about my planned adventure. They were unanimously terrified at the idea. They threatened to hide my bike and put me on a bus if I didn't change my mind. Not having yet been fully indoctrinated by the sport, I let them influence me and I wimped out of my first motorcycling adventure. My car-guy heart was holding me back.

I contacted one of those driveaway services that people with money use to take advantage of transients, like I then was. Poor suckers like me get to drive their cars across the USA while they fly their lazy, rich asses over it. One phone call later, I had reserved a car that needed to be reunited with its owner in a town about 30 miles from my hometown destination that was some 1,300 miles from Tampa. Not bad, no?

In the waiting room of where my assignment and I would meet, while waiting to be introduced to my temporary car, I read through the cars and their destinations listed on a chalkboard. I noticed a Yugo that needed some poor lost soul to drive it from Tampa to Seattle. Yes — Seattle, Washington. Three time zones west and basically a full continent away, in case you don't know your geography. That would be just about a cool 3,000 miles. I don't care what your economic status is, anyone connected with that deal is a loser. The owners should have burned the car before they fled west, and the person thinking of driving it there should hitchhike. Well, they would be hitchhiking soon enough.

I was led out to the parking lot and then handed the keys to my...BRAND NEW OLDSMOBILE DELTA 88 CONVERTIBLE! I won! I won!

Since I had hit pay dirt with the car, I committed to using it to transport all of my belongings — including my Honda CB350. I re-pulled the bike's engine, took off both wheels, pulled the front fork legs, and that was about it. I laid the frame in the trunk on its side and set the engine in the center of it vertically and then tucked the tank, seat and wheels into the spaces around the frame. It was surprisingly easy, even though I had a friend there who was supposed to help but instead spent the entire time telling me over and over that the bike wasn't going to fit. So if anyone ever asks you, yes, a complete Honda CB350 will fit into the trunk of a '78 Delta 88 convertible.

I hit the road. I'd planned on taking my jolly time, cruising cool roads through the Appalachians. But by the time I'd reached Georgia, I realized something was very wrong. The car smelled like gasoline and the car's mileage sucked. The fuel tank had sprung a leak.

I don't know if one of the many bumps in the road that the car's ass dragged over had ground a hole in it from below or what. But I knew that there was as much fuel coming out onto the road as there was being sucked down the throat of the car's giant four-barrel carb. Where the leak was didn't matter — all that mattered was going as fast as possible to maximize the mpg I could get out of a tankful of gas.

Thankfully, I made it all the way to New York state without having to experiment with whether or not it is possible to outrun flames. I dropped the car off at its owners after removing my stuff and any evidence of motorcycle cargo. The owner was so overjoyed to actually see his car with most major body panels still attached that I didn't want to unnecessarily concern him with details, so I split.

Once home, I immediately set to putting my bike back together for what would be the beginning of my Summer of Love. I was about to become a motorcyclist and there was no one who could stop me now.

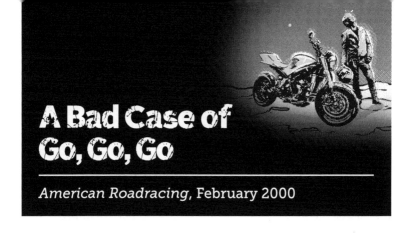

A Bad Case of Go, Go, Go

American Roadracing, February 2000

What is it with speed anyway? Does it cause some kind of addictive chemical reaction in some humans? It puzzles me why some of us have to go stinking fast, even if it's just to the grocery store. I am told that there are many who don't drive or ride every vehicle they can get their hands on as fast as they can possibly go. Weirder yet, I've heard that there are some who actually have a dislike of speed. So why is it that some of us can't resist hammering throttle stops?

I got to thinking about speed after seeing the "200 MPH Club" decals that Rick Yacoucci had on the tail-section of his motorcycle, earning them at Bonneville and El Mirage this year. Looking at them, all I could think about was getting a couple just like them for myself. Well, alright, maybe I already do have one. But I could use a couple more.

When I look back over my life, I realize that even as a child I was always looking for ways to generate speed. I loved it when my father passed other cars while he drove the family station wagon. I'll always remember the eight or nine times that it happened. Back in those days there weren't many four-lane roads, so passing took commitment and planning. There also weren't radial tires and rack-and-pinion steering on American-made station wagons. One car passing another back then was a heroic activity. The fact that my father did it at all with a family of nine in the car is pretty impressive. That's got to be well over a ton of meat. He did what he could.

The two houses we lived in while I was growing up were on hills. It hadn't dawned on me until just now the importance of that. Hills are a valuable commodity to a kid looking for speed. Hills are a child's source of horsepower, and environmentally friendly. For kids who live in cities, all of which generally don't allow children to operate vehicles with internal combustion engines, hills are particularly valuable.

In the summer we would drag anything with wheels to the top of our hill. We would then ride the things down. This included bicycles, push go-carts, wagons, shopping carts, tires, toy trucks large enough to sit on, and so on. In the winter we would drag sleds, boxes, boards, and those aluminum discs of death to the top of the hill. If there are any children reading this, let me give you a few pointers.

Have your dad get you a wagon with an actual steering rack. The ones with the solid front axle and a single pivot in the front-center of the wagon are bad news. The outer wheel on those moves to the middle of the wagon when trying to negotiate a turn, which causes nasty rollovers. Also, stay away from shopping carts. The reverse trail of the front wheels makes them unsafe at any speed, and Corvairs don't hold squat to those death traps. Plus, adding to the danger of their unsteerability is the fact that they're really hard to get out of while in motion. So they always end up on top of you when they flip. And they always do flip.

My last, and most serious, warning is about using a truck tire as a vehicle. Stay as far away from that idea as possible. One of the kids on my street dragged one up the hill, rolled his little body up inside it and let himself roll. Man, did he pick up speed quickly. He started screaming for help after about only seven feet of travel, but it was already too late. The problem with truck tires is the inverse of that with shopping carts. They're too damn stable and, once they get going, they will roll forever. Everyone took off running after him trying to kick him over and throwing stuff at him in an attempt to knock him down. Those efforts changed his direction slightly but nothing more. Within seconds, he was going faster than anyone could run and there was nothing left to do but watch. He would have set a distance and speed record had it not been for that tree. The kid was never quite the same after that.

From there I graduated to bigger bicycles, bigger hills, and eventually, of course, to things with motors. But all this seems very normal to me, and I can't say that I truly consider myself to be actually addicted to speed as if it were some kind of irrational dependency. Maybe. Sort of. I could be wrong.

It might be that I don't look at myself as a speed addict purely because I have a friend who is speed incarnate. Next to him, I'm just a benchwarmer. He goes fast everywhere and in every vehicle he can get his hands on. This friend has surrounded himself with speed. His cars, his bikes, his boat, his snowmobile, his four-wheeler… everything he owns is powered by the biggest, fastest engine that money can buy. Not only does he have a need for speed but also a full-blown phobia of slow.

When riding in a group with him, he is the one who hits the throttle the hardest first. The closest fun road to Syracuse is informally known as "13 Curves." That pretty well describes the reason we were there, except I think there are actually only 12 curves. But that number doesn't help the local folklore as much as 13 does. By day the road is for speed demons, by night it is for conventional demons.

We would ride up and down it repeatedly until our speeds built to the point that we started scaring even ourselves. The fact that the full length of the road was lined with guardrail on one side and the wall of a cliff on the other never seemed to mean much to us. Somehow we would stop before we became a part of the folklore and legend. Or at least we'd stop after the first crash of the day.

My primary vision of this friend will always be from many years ago when we passed each other while going in opposite directions. It was at the bottom of a mile-long climb he was about to make up a steep hill. At the time he was riding an '80s Kawasaki GPZ1100, and he was wearing an open-faced helmet. Just as I was nearing him, he whacked his bike's throttle wide open and it lurched forward, storming up the hill while he hung on tightly with his helmet rolling back on his head. He looked like a crazed Ed "Big Daddy" Roth hot rod character — all that was missing were the giant, popped-out bloodshot eyes. (Not that I haven't since seen him like that too.)

It was while riding with him and passing cars that I first learned of the secret motorcycle lane on highways. An oncoming car suddenly came into view from around a curve and made me look for a way back into my lane. But the line of cars I was passing didn't allow that. Just as I was about to grab a handful of brakes, I noticed the oncoming car veered to its right, giving me room. So I took the clue and pulled onto the centerline and continued passing the cars. It worked just fine. Country roads aren't two lanes wide, they are three lanes wide — two for cars and one for bikes right down the center.

I am lying. There really is no secret motorcycle lane. As soon as I tried the antic again, the driver of the car approaching panicked and swerved nearly out of control. I realized then that I was a terror of the highways. I realized then that I needed to get myself to a racetrack before innocent people died.

I didn't go racing until I was in my mid-30s, a couple years after this incident. Although some might think racing is dangerous, in my case it was much safer than the alternative.

The primary reason to go racing is to keep from killing or hurting other people. Racing reduces risk, it doesn't increase it. The shocker that comes to most who begin racing is how much it immediately slows them down on the street. Going fast on the street becomes less fun because racing reveals it instantly as a fast that's much slower than can be experienced on a racetrack, while being six times more dangerous.

So alright, I give up: My name is Peter. I'm a speedaholic.

For those still in denial of a speed addiction, I've come up with a simple test to determine whether or not you're a speed addict. If you answer yes to the following three questions, report to your nearest racing facility immediately:

1) Are 90% of your scars the result of speed-related activities? 2) Have you unofficially top-speed tested every vehicle you've ever owned? 3) Are you reading a magazine about motorcycles and racing?

Gimmie Them Gs

American Roadracing, February 2000

I have already confessed to a personal addiction to speed, but I'm having second thoughts. I think I might have misdiagnosed a symptom as being a sickness. It might not be speed that is my addiction. No, it might actually be the achieving of speed that is my addiction. In other words: G-forces — the hasty violation of inertia.

Thinking back over my life's experiences with speed, I'm beginning to realize that it's not so much the ultimate top speed reached that makes me all giggly inside. It's more the speed at which that speed is reached. It isn't so much the going fast that speed freaks like me desire. It's the getting to fast as quickly as possible that we can't resist. It's not the fast, it's the going faster fast. It's an easy thing to get confused about, no? So speed freaks might be an incorrect appellation. It should be "G-freaks."

Part of my confusion about the object of my true addiction might be due to how society at large is generally confused over how humans are affected by speed and G-forces. When people who are not involved in motorsports find out what I do for a living, they ask just one question: "What's the fastest you've ever gone on a motorcycle?" I am never asked what is the quickest I've ever accelerated. Motor vehicles don't come with G-meters, so no one has any baseline for inquiry.

People are very impressed when I tell them how fast I've gone, even though they've all gone faster. There are trains in a number of countries that go well-over 200 mph. Passenger planes regularly fly at over 300 mph. In today's world, it's getting hard to find anyone who hasn't ridden in a jet-powered vehicle. So why all these questions about speed? When those vehicles are operating correctly, there is no thrill in riding in them. Their speed is accepted with nonchalance, an alcoholic beverage, and a nap.

In my early experiences with G-forces, I remember the times that my father floored the family wagon, passing Nash Metropolitans, overloaded dump trucks, and the Amish. But now that I think about those times, I realize they weren't really thrilling because we would achieve the rare speed of 75 mph or so. No, they were thrilling because father's right foot was pushing hard on the gas pedal and the wood-sided Ford wagon was accelerating with a burst of power that planted us firmly in our seats, comparatively speaking. Acceleration is a physical sensation. You can feel it with your eyes closed. Speed? Right now we're all going about 10,000 mph through space while rotating at about 1,000 mph. Again, who feels it? Who cares? But if we suddenly sped up to 15,000 mph... well, that'd be cool. We would notice that. That thought reminds me of a Tom Waits song, *"Earth Died Screaming."*

When my father would pass other vehicles, part of the thrill was to watch the speedometer sweep higher at a rate like a second hand on a clock, rather than the big hand's slow sweep barely undetectable to the naked eye. Once or twice, I think I even heard the extra throats of the four-barrel carbs actually kick open. While sitting in the back seat, I would press my right foot hard to the floor, trying to help out. Go daddy, go.

When I was about 14 years old, one of my brothers was driving the family wagon when he fulfilled an urge we each had never discussed: The urge to actually push that damn gas pedal to the floor with conviction and urgency. Our father had bought an American Motors Ambassador wagon with the full towing package. Since AMC didn't have a lot of engines to choose from, it tossed its "Machine" power plant into the loaded wagon. The "Machine" was AMC's muscle car. So under the hood of that wagon, with its fake wood trim, was a giant V-8 with chromed valve covers. A sleeper.

My brother Eric was driving the car while some slow-going road hog was getting on my brother's nerves. So he pulled out to pass the guy who then noticed this and accelerated. If my father, or any other truly responsible adult had been driving our car, this is where they would have let off the throttle and given up the attempt. But to my brother — and to me — this invitation, this slim excuse, was an opportunity to give that V-8 a self-realizing experience, allowing it to express its hot-rod soul. My brother stomped the gas pedal flat to the floor.

That car was pretty freaking fast, for a station wagon. In a sudden cloud of black smoke and piston carbon, the Ambassador roared forward quicker than I had ever experienced. That was the exact moment in my life when I felt the value of large bores and huge amounts of hydrocarbons dumping down the throats of an internal combustion engine with chromed valve covers. Horsepower good. This was a small event, yet I still remember and appreciate it some 30 years later. Why is that?

The problem with seeking G-forces through the power provided by internal combustion engines is that it costs a lot of money. But, as you probably also realized, motorcycles don't cost as much as cars do to accelerate at a visceral rate. That knowledge is probably what has led you to reading this magazine. It's also something that we try not to advertise to the nonmotorcycling community. You and I know that they wouldn't understand.

Most people, even though they do not race or operate high-performance vehicles, share this attraction to G-forces. I know this because there are places all over the country that make millions of dollars each year by selling G-forces. They're called amusement parks. Every ride that I can think of in those parks is designed with the primary purpose of generating G-forces. Or, to enhance the experience, the rides generate high G's then take it all away as quickly as possible. Negative Gs are almost as satisfying as piled on loads of Gs. Roller coasters, Tilt-a-Whirls, teacups, that swinging ship thing, and so on, all offer Gs in slightly different packages. Many of these rides spin because centrifugal force is a great way to create Gs in the convenience of a confined circle. And now there's the very popular ultimate G-force thrill...bungee jumping.

My father was a responsible guy, so he wouldn't accelerate at a rate that was unnecessary to the act of transporting our family. But he did indulge us in other automotive G-thrills. There was a road we often traveled that had a number of particularly steep little rolling hills. When traveled fast enough, a car would nearly fly off the top of them, bottoming out in the small valleys between. No Gs, lots of Gs, no Gs, lots of Gs, no Gs, lots of Gs.... We loved that road because our father would drive it fast enough to make it meaningful.

I tried out the sport of luge a few years ago. But while doing it, I kept slamming nearly head-on and hard into the opposite wall when exiting the tight turns. The faster I went, the harder I would hit those walls. This perplexed me because I couldn't stop doing it. I eventually realized that the reason I was hitting those walls was because I was staying up on the vertical banking of the turns way too long. I was unconsciously trying to maximize my time in the corner in order to feel the most Gs possible. Once I figured that out, I steered down properly and stopped hitting the walls. But it was quite hard to give up those Gs. But seeking Gs is why I was on a luge course to begin with.

Who doesn't remember the sensation of their first ride at the controls of a motorcycle? The rush, the shocking surge forward, the feeling in the stomach, the uncontrollable laughter — all from just twisting the throttle. There is no other vehicle that connects the operator so closely with its power. There is nothing else that comes close to equaling the feeling that a motorcycle gives of being hurtled face first through space. Having the engine between your legs makes it that much better. In total, it is the nearest thing to saddling up a rocket. And who among us doesn't long for that?

So I'm now convinced that G-forces are the major attraction of riding a motorcycle down a canyon road. Hard braking creates Gs, accelerating hard creates Gs, and cornering creates Gs. A tight road is a G-force festival. The tighter the road the better, because it generates Gs even at a reasonable speed. On a tight road 40 mph can feel fast because with big Gs ultimate speed doesn't matter. Speed isn't the thrill, it's the getting speed quickly that matters. It's the launch and the acceleration.

For the dollar, is there any G-force generator that comes even close to a motorcycle? Um, no. Motorcycles are an amusement park on two wheels that fits in your garage. Horsepower good. Motorcycles great.

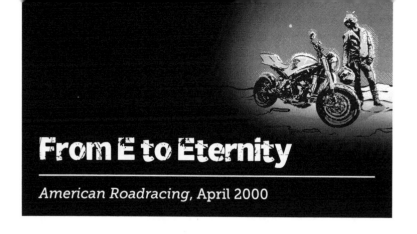

From E to Eternity

American Roadracing, April 2000

Did you ever leave your house in the morning only to realize halfway to work that you forgot to turn off your coffee maker? Yeah, me too. Why is that?

Did you ever promise your significant other that you'd meet her somewhere and, an hour after you were supposed to be there, suddenly go flush with panic when you realize why that woman wasn't with you right then? Me too. Why is that?

Some things in life seem almost impossible to forget, while other things are much too easily forgotten. Furthermore, some things are virtually impossible to remember. In trying to understand this phenomenon, I've come to realize that the level of importance of something has nothing to do with remembering it.

In trying to understand this human foible, I've come to realize that the question shouldn't be: Why do we forget some things? But instead: Why do we often remember things? The inquiry is backward. Forgetting is normal. Forgetting is the default position of the human brain. Forgetting is soothing; a lazy brain doesn't consider consequences. So I am no longer stunned by my ability to forget. Instead, I am stunned at times by my ability to actually remember. What's this got to do with motorcycles?

Gas gauges, that's what.

I have run out of gas on every motorcycle I've ever owned. Actually, I've run out of gas while driving every vehicle I've ever owned and many that I've borrowed or rented. Some do think that this is strange. I, of course, think that this is normal. Which is why the new trend of putting gauges on motorcycles is, to me, a wasted effort. I'll forget to look at them.

I ran out of gas once, on my Honda CB350, while on the way home from a girlfriend's house. I ran out of gas in Iowa City on my CB400FSupersport. I ran out of gas on a rainy night in the Adirondack Mountains on my Ducati 860. I convinced my racing partner not to check the fuel level before his first race, and he ran out of gas during his race. Apparently, I share my mastered ability of running out of gas. I also ran out of gas in a lonely part of Oklahoma on my move to the West Coast to set up this office. And so on. But that last one wasn't my fault. Really. The others, yes, but not that one.

When I went motorcycle racing and had to transport bikes all over the country, I quickly learned the secondary use of race bikes: an emergency fuel source. In my years of racing and running a race team, I don't think there's a single race bike that I didn't eventually pull the tank off of while on the side of some highway to drain its fuel into our stalled van or tow vehicle. I once considered getting a map of the country and marking all of these sites where I have run out of gas with pushpins. But that would be sort of like Napoleon marking off his march of failure from Russia to France. Am I being melodramatic?

People who travel with me have learned to watch the fuel gauge after I point out to them a few of the places where I've run out of gas. People are effective gas gauges. Especially the one(s) you marry.

Some of my friends think this flaw of mine is strange. I think they're strange. But then again, maybe it is a learning disability, or something. Hell, it's been nearly a week since I last ran a vehicle out of gas. I wish I were joking. So as far as I'm concerned, the concept of fuel gauges is totally whacked. If I'm not going to think about gas, I'm not going to think about looking at a fuel gauge either. Every time I catch one that is reading near empty out of the corner of my eye, it is purely by accident. And now the things are popping up on motorcycles — like that's going to help me?

I've read that humans tend to organize thoughts by leaving trivial information out of their minds. But what is trivial is often a matter of context; sometimes gasoline is trivial, and sometimes it isn't. If one's motorcycle tank is full of gas, then gasoline is trivial. So, at that point it's not normal to reflect deeply about how pleasant it is to have gasoline in your tank. Gasoline is automatically supposed to become nontrivial when we're in need of some. Fair enough. I can agree with that. But the only way to know if you're in need of some is if you happen to look at the fuel gauge, or if the bike you're riding stops running and you have to turn the petcock to reserve. The problem is having the ability to understand when the trivial is no longer trivial.

Did I say "petcock"? The old-timey second chance. I miss those things.

And there is another problem.

Maybe it is genes, but maybe it is a cultural thing. Even if I do happen to notice that the bike I'm riding has a gauge reading "E," I don't necessarily believe that it is time to fuel up. For a whole culture of people like me, "E" means, "Enough." "E" means, "Don't cross a desert but otherwise don't worry about it." "E" means, "I wonder how much farther I can go?" Running out of gas is a measure of limits. It's a pushing of the envelope. It's a dare gone wrong; an accidental adventure.

So gas gauges don't serve any purpose for me because I don't look at them. And when I accidentally do, I act badly. And petcocks fail me because the reserve on bikes is usually much too large, so I have to time to forget twice. When a bike stumbles out of fuel and I turn a petcock to reserve, it means that I need to try to remember to get gas at some, as yet not quite defined, future moment. Maybe tomorrow. Maybe. Needing gas became nontrivial for a moment and, once I pivot a petcock to reserve, it becomes trivial again.

Maybe with motorcycles I doubt fuel gauges because of my experiences of removing a bike's gas tank and shaking trapped gas into the lines and then driving on. There's always some. That's not an easy task with a car's gas tank. And with bikes you can always just take a look inside and make you own decision. Again, with cars you can't do that. Of course with EFI you can no longer do it with many motorcycles either.

So, again: Gas gauges on bikes? What do I care? I'll still run out of gas.

But clocks? I love today's trend of having clocks on motorcycles. They provide a running measure of exactly how late I am. And exactly what time it is when I run out of gas.

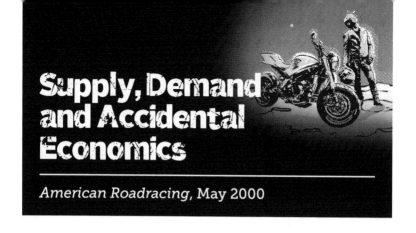

Supply, Demand and Accidental Economics

American Roadracing, May 2000

The name of that film, *"The Accidental Tourist,"* bugged me. I can't figure out what the hell it is supposed to mean. How could anyone be a tourist by accident? That's silly. I wondered for a while if it hadn't something to do with that old joke: "Have a nice 'trip,' see you next 'fall.'" But that seemed a little too simpleminded.

Because of a personal experience that I had last month, I now completely understand what that title is about. I recently went to Daytona Bike Week...by accident. And by that I don't mean that by accident I went to Daytona to cover the motorcycle racing at the Daytona International Speedway. That was on purpose. It's the being there for Bike Week part that was inadvertent.

This realization came to me at Daytona when l was woken up in the middle of the night, for the fifth night in a row. Someone was revving the hell out of a mufflerless V-twin cruiser in our hotel parking lot. I looked over at snoring Blake Conner, the Art Director of *American Roadracing*, and couldn't believe he was sleeping through the hearing-damaging noise. I then remembered that he was wearing earplugs.

(That reminds me, on one of those nights I was woken up by Blake yelling in his sleep. Blake has a history of talking in his sleep, but at Daytona he had to yell in his sleep because otherwise he couldn't hear his own somnambulic mutterings while wearing earplugs. I could have worn them too, but earplugs interfere with my sleep more than the occasional motorcyclist blasting the paint off the walls of our room.)

Anyway, lying awake and frustrated, I started wondering what I was doing at Daytona with tens of thousands of cruiser, chopper, bobber, V-twin, push-rod bikers. Don't get me wrong. It's not that I have anything against those bikes; it's just that we were not attending a cruiser event. We were attending a roadracing event. That's when I realized that...wait a minute...yes, we were attending a cruiser event and just because no one had ever explained that to me doesn't change the facts.

A revealing light went off in my head and I finally realized that those silly little races over at the Daytona International Speedway were really nothing more than a sideshow to the other activities going on around Daytona during Bike Week. Sure, to racing enthusiasts, the roadracing is important, but most of the motorcyclists in Daytona aren't roadracing enthusiasts. Roadraces, including the Daytona 200, are not why Bike Week still exists today and not why most motorcyclists go to Daytona. As much as I'd not like to think it, if there was no Daytona 200 in 2001, there would still be a Bike Week.

Some 60 years ago, when the Daytona 200 was founded, racers and motorcycle enthusiasts went to Daytona to participate in or watch the racing. But the event has evolved and, over more than a half-century since its inception, there have been a few wars, nearly all of the American motorcycle companies have gone out of business, the motorcycle industry has grown, shrunk, grown again, then upside-down forks were invented, and the motorcycle event at Daytona has gone in two highly different and separate directions.

Today, of the large number of motorcyclists who go to Bike Week only a very small percentage of them ever go into the Daytona International Speedway. To most bikers, Bike Week is a giant cruiser, V-twin bike party — just like Sturgis, SD, and Laconia, NH. The fact that it coincides with motorcycle racing at the Daytona International Speedway is now nothing more than an accident of history. In contrast, during Speed Week, which is for cars, all of the activities revolve around the NASCAR racing. During Bike Week, the racing is just another of many, many attractions. The swap meet, coleslaw wrestling, wall of death, leather-bra vendors, and so on, all have as much or more pertinence to Bike Week than the racing at the Daytona International Speedway.

Sportbike guys and cruiser guys don't hang out together, don't understand each other, don't live in the same culture, and don't share the same enthusiasms. Well, some do but most don't. We asked a few of the bikers staying in the same hotel as us that was located directly across the street from the Daytona International Speedway whether or not they were going to attend the races. The primary response we got was a blank stare followed by: "What races?"

On Main Street, over at the beach where the 200,000 cruiser riders hang out, the answer was the same: "What races?" Or some will say, "You mean the dirt-track stuff at the fairgrounds?"

But the noise, the crowds, the stinky exhaust, all of those things are not the worst part about being at Bike Week by accident. In fact, in moderation most of that stuff is actually enjoyable. I am a motorcyclist after all. The thing that truly does suck is the hotel bill. In 1996, when I last had a racing team, we competed at the Daytona International Speedway during Bike Week. And one hotel I called for reservations that year wanted $185 a night per room. Three rooms at that place for 11 nights was going to be about equal to our hotel expenses for the rest of the racing season.

That year the Daytona 200 was rained out so we had to return to race a week later after Bike Week was over. I called that same hotel and the price per night, per room was $39.95. I'm not complaining about jacked-up hotel prices in general, which happens during popular events. That's how a free economy works. What is annoying is paying those jackedup prices for an event I'm not actually attending. That's why it's my habit not to vacation in Indianapolis during a Shriners convention. Or Lancaster, PA, during a barn-raising.

If the Daytona 200 was moved to a time other than Bike Week, I'm betting it would have more participants and more spectators. I bet that racing enthusiasts, who are smarter than me, years ago saw the silliness of being robbed by hotels just to see a race during a cruiser convention. The rained-out year, 1996, gave proof that the Daytona 200 doesn't increase hotel prices.

I would like to go to Bike Week again sometime to hang with the cruiser crowd. It's just that I want to do it on purpose.

Where's my Cigar?

American Roadracing, June 2000

What is this motorcycle enthusiast stuff all about anyway? Sometimes I wonder if we're not just a bunch of confused nerds. It's easy to point at the weirdness of those with fanatical devotion to a television show, but is there really a difference between fanatical enthusiasms? Sure, motor-powered, two-wheeled vehicles take devotion to operate properly. But when we say things like: "I got into a headshake, losing my footing on the rearsets, and thankfully it smoothed out so I didn't highside." Who but us knows what we're talking about?

All in all, it seems that a dedicated enthusiasm for any healthy activity is a perfectly normal human behavior. It's just that other people's enthusiasm for things that you're not enthusiastic about is weird. My suspicion is that every normal person has a special enthusiastic interest in something. And, as a nation, we have just silently agreed to pick on Trekkies for their hobby because they are the easiest to make fun of. We can all rest assured that no matter how peculiar our interests may appear to be, at least they don't include dressing up in silly costumes, taking trips to big gatherings, speaking in a secret language, and...oh, wait a minute... never mind.

Once, some nonmotorcyclist asked me something about the top speed of the bike I was riding. Out of appreciation of the question and wanting to give him a quality answer, I started telling him about countersteering, *"Easy Rider,"* T.E. Lawrence, helmet laws, the history of Laconia, and 90- versus 45-degree V-twins. I was barely into giving him some of the most critically necessary and interesting information about motorcycles when I noticed that he had suddenly broken out in a cold sweat and his eyes rolled up into his head.

Conversely, once I happened to ask a guy what year his Monte Carlo was. He started describing each and every detail of every year's model changes of the car — from year one up through 2008, and then he somehow segued into a dissertation of Dale Earnhardt's racing career beginning with the first date of Dale's parents. Starting at about 30 seconds into his diatribe, I was praying for death.

These two experiences revealed to me the definition of hobby vs. dedicated enthusiasm. In a nutshell, dedicated enthusiasm is a devotion so powerful that a human will voluntarily dedicate every available spare waking minute to it, while the person sitting next to them would rather die than hear about it. Yet, as long as there are at least two other people in the world who share that enthusiasm, that person is possibly normal. This is hard to measure because everyone has to hide their hobby from someone, "You play with trains? Ha, ha, ha." Mean people say things like that.

It hadn't dawned on me until some years after becoming a motorcycle enthusiast that being one was anything special. I just liked bikes and gradually started having more and more to do with them, that's all. My attraction was controlled and moderate.

I knew that I wasn't any sort of addict and I could quit anytime I wanted to.

After being involved in this sport for a couple of years, I was hanging out at a bike shop one day, simply because hanging out at a bike shop is the right thing to do. While leaving that shop, I noticed that no one was hanging out at the hardware store across the street. That hardware store had some mighty fine products, such as lawn mowers and toaster ovens and shovels and stuff, but the only people who walked through its doors were customers who were there for the purpose of making a purchase. Not a single one of them was leaning against the counter in the garden section admiring the new Mower Spectacular 3000 while mulling over powerful thoughts regarding what cool aftermarket parts he could bolt to the machine or whether or not its chromed plastic wheels were just a passing fad.

Meanwhile, my involuntary trips to fabric stores back then had revealed very serious and concerned discussions some women have concerning choosing the proper thread colors and stitch pattern for a log-cabin quilt they're making for the spring quilt show. I don't actually understand any of this paragraph.

I have been wondering about this stuff and what it means to be a motorcycle enthusiast because sometimes some bikers seem to enjoy taking their enthusiasms to exclusionary extremes. There are Ducati enthusiasts who wouldn't be caught dead standing anywhere near something as horrid as a 90-degree V-twin with belt-driven cams. For them, it's gotta be a bevel drive or it's not a "real" Ducati. There are two-stroke enthusiasts who yell obscenities at every four-stroke bike they see. There are people who ride Moto Guzzis. Talk about weird. Which reminds me: What's up with those BMW guys who all wear reflective vests, use hand signals, and have great posture?

All said, I am not specific in my motorcycle enthusiasm. I embrace every motorized two-wheeled vehicle on the planet. Some of you might think less of me for that, but so be it. I like knowing the difference between an H-D owner who is a weekend warrior and one who is an old-school biker. The first of those rides an Evolution-engined machine, while the second will know you're a pretender if you ask him what year his bike is. Any "real" Harley is a conglomeration of many years' worth of parts.

I own a '62 Vespa. I like vintage racing and dream of owning a Brough Superior. I know that Steve McQueen rode a Triumph in *"The Great Escape."* And I love the looks of the new Benelli that has some performance issues. OK, I'm just showing off now.

I do know that a guy riding a scooter because it's cheap transportation is not an enthusiast, and he will not wave at another bike. While someone riding a scooter because he thinks it's cool is an enthusiast and wants to wave but knows not to. It's not the vehicle that matters, it's the rider's state of mind. So I chance waving to people on scooters.

My point is: I love all bikes from scooters to cruisers to sportbikes to whatever. You might not, and that's great too. I don't think that all bikers should love all bikes and love all other bikers. Some do, some don't, and that's what makes life interesting. Just don't be a Trekkie.

The Price of Freedom

Motorcycle Street & Strip,
September/October 2000

A s with likely most of you, my love for motorcycles has much to do with the fact that they have engines. Sure, having that engine between my knees and sitting in the wind each also have something to do with it, but the engine is the key to the experience. I mention this because I'm now thinking of buying a bicycle. As you know, they don't have engines. I am tormented.

It's not that I don't like bicycles. It's that I really, sincerely, truly do not like them. I'm not on the fence about this. Bicycles are to motorcycles what mobile homes are to houses. They're what waving a sign on a street corner is to having a job. They're what radio is to TV. They're … well, you get the picture. Whenever I pass someone riding a bicycle, I'm always tempted to yell at them, "Get an engine!"

When I was a kid, a bicycle was my primary source of long-distance autonomous transportation. But, from day one, I considered that an unfortunate and unfair fact of life. I used a bicycle to go places not because I enjoyed the thrill of piloting a human-powered vehicle, but because it was all that I was allowed by law to pilot. I was victim of The Man. I wanted an engine. I ached to have an engine. So what if I was only 11 years old?

Adding to my sorry torment was the fact that my parents always bought houses on the tops of hills. When they moved us to the suburbs, where nothing that a child's heart desires is within walking distance, they managed to find a house on top of a hill that was on top of a hill. From there, each of my bicycling adventures ended with me dragging my bike back up steep hills, having to pay back all of the gravity I'd taken advantage of during each journey's beginning. I've forgotten how many times I considered chucking my bicycle into the bushes and walking home without it. As cars and trucks and motorcycles sped by me, I schemed and dreamed about getting an engine.

Many of my childhood days on a bicycle were spent pretending that I wasn't on a bicycle, and that I wasn't a kid. When my buddies and I would build a ramp to jump in an empty lot, we didn't think of ourselves as kids jumping a ramp in an empty lot. We were Steve McQueen on a motorcycle, railing across rolling hills at the foot of the Alps, jumping the barbed-wire fence that stood between us and freedom.

It's all of those human-powered moments of riding a bicycle that I hated, not the moments of gravity-powered riding. Riding a bicycle is like doing manual labor for free. It's slavery. I spent my teen years staring longingly out my bedroom window at a highway in the distance, watching engine-powered vehicles fly by, daydreaming about one day owning one of those vehicles. For me, the internal combustion engine represented freedom. An engine was my Moses, leading me to my promised land. If I had one, I could go farther faster and for longer than I'd ever gone on a bicycle. If I had an engine, I could go anywhere at any time.

I once worked at a giant publishing house that had its bicycle and motorcycle magazine staff offices within the same production area. To me, that combination made as much sense as having Teen Vogue and Gun Digest share an office space. Having two wheels, like having two legs, does not in and of itself bond men. Us motorcycle editors would ride motorcycles to work while the bicycle guys showed up on their bicycles. The motored half of us wore leather; the pedaling half wore spandex and performance underpants. The motored group has a storied bad-boy history; the pedalers had spent their teen years delivering newspapers and groceries. There is no common bond between bikers and bicyclers.

It took me a few months of working there before I finally realized that the bicyclists in the office didn't ride bicycles wholly and only because they had each been denied driver's licenses. They actually, on purpose, chose to ride bicycles voluntarily — and enjoyed it. They talked bicycle talk during lunch. They rode bicycles on weekends in their spare time.

So, with all this said, why am I now shopping for a bicycle? It's because the aging process has altered my metabolism and now I have to actually spend time doing what my physiology used to do automatically all by itself. I used to be able to eat as much as I wanted, never needing to worry about the consequences. There weren't any. Until recently, I had never weighed more than 145 pounds at any time in my life. I was a 98-pound weakling until I was 22 years old. Today I've swollen into a 160-pound weakling.

Now when I eat, my body only uses half of the food and stores the other half. It stores it all below my ribs and above my pelvis; all in a pile swelling from my midsection. I guess this is normal. At first, I thought that all of my pants were shrinking, but then I inadvertently caught the reflection of my profile in a store window:

bad posture, bulging gut. There was no more denying it. I now know that middle age doesn't refer to a time in one's life. It refers to an event in one's life. It's when everything that you eat comes to collect in your middle, like silt on a river's curve.

I could try some other program of carbohydrate burning, something modern like Pilates, or P90X, or CrossFit, or whatever that thing is that Texas Ranger Walker is promoting. But the threat of boredom encourages me to become a bicyclist. On a bicycle I can at least experience the spontaneity of seeing new things. I can take part in the world outside of my house, enjoy the weather, and go to some destination while I'm exercising — like to a coffee shop where they serve mocha lattes.

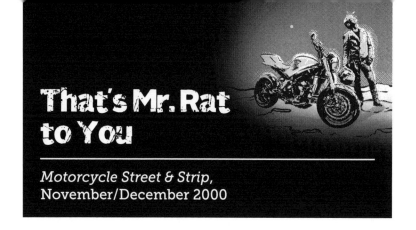

That's Mr. Rat to You

Motorcycle Street & Strip,
November/December 2000

N ew bikes are cool. Maybe I can even afford one. I think the main reason I was a reader of motorcycle magazines before finally becoming an editor is because I have so rarely been able to. I don't mean read; I mean afford a new bike.

Bike magazines are kind of like some movies: They let us share in experiencing things that we might not be able to experience personally: like being in a car chase through San Francisco, or saving the planet from attacking aliens, or making love to Russian spies who somehow always look more like supermodels than civil servants, or riding expensive and exotic motorcycles.

There are, I'm told, those who read motorcycle magazines because they are actually planning on buying a motorcycle. Every day, I pretend that I know this even though I find it difficult to empathize with those readers. But I do know that, for most enthusiasts, it's often difficult to personally test ride different bikes. So published road tests and the opinions of journalists are often all there is to go by before making a very expensive decision, and hopefully not a costly one. I'm told that's basically the real function of a motorcycle magazine: to connect the readers to the products. And, actual buyers or dreamers, it's all the same, I guess. A dreamer is just a future buyer. Or so we dreamers keep telling ourselves.

It's because of my personal experience of starting out my motorcycling passion with modest funds that I will always treat the rat bike owner with respect. Sometimes, a rat bike is all a rider can afford. And, in those cases, one has to be careful about using the word "rat" while referring to that bike in front of its owner. That would be like telling a mom her baby is ugly. There's a big difference between bikes that are rats, and bikes that look like rats but whose owners don't think of them as such. Often the only way to tell these two types of bikes from each other is by how the latter of the two look like washed and combed rats, so to speak. To be safe, just do what I did and memorize these two lines, "Wow, what a pretty baby. Nice bike, dude."

Like half of the enthusiasts my age, my first street bike was a Honda CB350. It wasn't new when I bought it. It wasn't used when I bought it, either. It was used up. So I rebuilt it (not very well) and repainted it with a spray can or two from the local hardware store (very well, if I say so myself), and I was a motorcyclist. And that bike was fast…well, in its day, compared to my father's 610 Datsun. I didn't even have to downshift while going up most hills.

In those early days, my helmet was an openfaced thing and my racing friends and the magazines made me lust for a Bell X-1. I think it was an X-1. Or was that the name of that spacecraft that those puppets rode around in on that TV show, the name of which I can't remember either? Whatever. Most of all, I lusted for a real leather motorcycle jacket. And, an aftermarket slip-on to replace the right muffler whose end was rotted out. When I finally had $150 in my pocket, I had to make a decision: muffler, jacket, muffler, jacket, muffler, jacket …. I'm pretending. The choice was

106

easy because only one of those items came with "cool." I sawed both stock mufflers in half so they'd match.

Nothing says "rebel motorcyclist" more than a leather jacket. Wearing the thing while riding made me feel both cool and invincible. The wind no longer went through me. Bugs were no longer feared.

Since I was a cafe racer kind of guy, the next purchase I made was a set of Clubman handlebars. For you kids out there, in the old days only one or two companies in the world made clip-ons. And generally, every motorcycle had actual handlebars, like a bicycle. Really. Installing a set of clipons was problematic because the headlight mounting brackets back then always completely filled the space between the upper and lower triple clamps. Clubman bars could be mounted like conventional handlebars and they curved down at each end rather than up, putting the bar ends where sportbike clip-ons are now. With that modification, voila, my CB350 was a sportbike.

So I rode my 350 like it was a sportbike and entertained my friends and myself by dragging the footpeg mounts around corners. It seemed daring at the time and, considering the suspect rubber that was mounted on the bike, it very well could have been.

I've come to think that it's during that formative stage of a rider's motorcycling experience that an enthusiast becomes either captivated by road racing or drag racing. It's a question of economics. Riding at idiot speeds through turns is cheap. Blowing everyone away at traffic lights costs money. So, since I didn't have many expendable funds early on, when I finally did have some money it was time to go road racing. The result of that was, of course, once again having no money. Maybe now that I'm at this magazine I should go get another CB350 and start all over. This time, since I've already got a leather jacket and some spare change, I could put my money into installing a big-bore kit and a nitrous system on it. Yeah, that'd be cool. Is there a rat ET class?

For Sale: GSX-R1000, Slow!

Motorcycle Street & Strip,
January/February 2001

How fast is fast? I've been pondering this for years. I read about fast in motorcycle magazines and on websites all the time, especially when it's in reference to a bike for sale. "1978 Kawasaki 450, fast!" Or, "1996 Yamaha YZF600, very fast!" It's often difficult to find a bike for sale that's not fast.

I've made the claim myself when selling a bike. I once advertised a '74 Yamaha RD350 as "fast." But the thing is, that bike was fast. At least it was in 1982 when I sold it. Its previous owner prior to me had raced it, and the engine was modified in some mysterious way that made the bike a beast of speed at the sacrifice of miles per gallon. It got, maybe, 11 of them. Possibly 12. Doubting that I could find anyone as foolish as myself to be interested in owning a motorcycle whose fuel-burning ability rivaled that of a Buick Delta 88, I tried skirting the issue by promoting the bike's one asset: It's fast.

The first person to come look at it was a 19-year-old prospective buyer. I allowed him to ride it about a half block in one direction, to where the street ended. But when he turned around and came back by me, he was doing about 80 mph. Thankfully my cat was in the house.

Moments later he returned screaming from his helmet, "Man, this bike is fast!" I knew the bike was sold, but I wanted to be an honest salesman so I quickly mentioned that it had very bad mileage. He didn't care.

I once met an owner of a vintage Moto Morini 500, who had industriously modified his bike to improve its performance. He told me it was the fastest Moto Morini in America. It fascinated me to learn that there was even one guy on the continent who truly believed that Moto Morini and "fastest" had ever glanced at each other in the hallway, forget about ever being introduced. He pointed out to me the new set of 26mm Dellorto carbs he'd installed in place of his bike's original 24mm units. I involuntarily blurted out, "Wow!" I was immediately embarrassed that he'd be hurt by my incredulous exclamation upon learning that Dellorto actually made carbs that small. Thankfully, he misinterpreted my spontaneous outburst as evidence of how impressed I was by his horsepower-boosting modification.

I once owned a Honda CB400F that shook its head violently at around an indicated 100 mph. Because of that, 100 mph on that bike felt very, very, very fast. At the time, I had a number of riding friends with 1000cc motorcycles. They often talked about how they wished their bikes were faster. I feigned agreement, secretly hoping not to die on my bike that seemed so slow to them.

A rider who was being paid by a manufacturer to road race its big-bore sportbike, once told me in confidence that the bike frightened the crap out of him. It didn't weave, it didn't have a head shake, it just didn't have any feel in its front end and it would toss him to the pavement unpredictably. Did that make this bike fast? Yes, it made it very, very, way too fast. But in context of the brands he was racing against and losing to, the bike was also way too slow.

In the early 1990s, four-time 500cc World Champion Eddie Lawson came out to compete in the Daytona 200 after a year's retirement. When asked during qualifying how it was going, he responded, "Things are finally beginning to slow down." After a year of being off a Grand Prix race bike, a slower Superbike had come to feel fast to Lawson. By race time, he'd sped his head up, slowing down the world around him, winning the Daytona 200 in 1993.

I used to top-speed test new production motorcycles back before the manufacturers secretly agreed to limit the top speed of their biggest bikes to 184 mph. (Don't tell them I told you that.) One bike I rode floated and weaved at speeds above 170 mph. At that speed it felt disconnected from the pavement, floating over it. Another bike I tested that same day was planted and easily controlled at over 180 mph, making that second motorcycle feel much slower. From that experience I wondered if maybe top-speed testing shouldn't concern itself with what the radar gun says, but instead with how the bike makes the rider feel at top speed.

Among the bikes I own today is a Honda CB200. Its front brake is a mechanically operated caliper. The pads within it that clamp against the rotor are glazed. So in effect I have a bike with inadequate stopping technology that has aged into an increased ineffectiveness. Its tires have been equally aged into ineffectiveness and their greatest risk of failure I'd guess is more from shattering than puncturing. Riding that bike down a moderate hill in second gear is an experience of fast at its most terrifying.

The result of all this is to say I've learned that fast is not a number or a matter of physics, it's a state of mind. And that state of mind is determined by the quality of control and feel a rider has of the motorcycle he's riding, not by what the speedometer says. The problem with speed is: The bikes that perform the best due to the confidence they inspire generally leave the impression of being the slowest, while the bikes that perform the worst feel the fastest.

This can be witnessed at any motorcycle roadracing event, particularly in today's MotoGP where setup is critical. As per the last paragraph, a racer who won last weekend and finished sixth this weekend invariably won on a slow bike and lost on a fast one. What I mean is, he won because everything was right, or near perfectly right. When he finished sixth, his bike was a beast. And he was likely riding harder than when he won, taking more chances, nearly crashing, and feeling as if he was straining to control a monster that wanted to kill him. Races tend to be won at the slowest pace that the winner can manage and are lost by everyone else riding as fast as possible.

Champions, Cheaters and Chumps

Motorcycle Street & Strip,
March/April 2001

R ecently, a sponsored rider who had just finished his first track test on a brand-new 600 Supersport bike was quoted in a news item happily exclaiming, "My lap times were just as low as with last year's bike and this engine is still stock!"

Hmmm …. What does he mean? Aren't Supersport engines always stock?

When I had a road racing team, we won many championships in the WERA National Endurance Series with bikes that fulfilled every letter of the rules. But when we first went "pro" racing, Supersport racing, most of our competitors' bikes were stupid-fast compared to ours. Were they cheating? Were we stupid-slow?

As a child, I had some friends who were really bad losers and they would scream and cry whenever they lost. To reduce their pain — and more importantly, mine — I started cheating when playing games with them to make sure I'd lose. They never noticed. Who would? But I never cheated to win, probably because my parents were both moral maniacs. There's no recording how many times 1 had heard the admonishment from my mother, "Just because you don't get caught, doesn't mean it's not wrong."

My father, on the other hand, had a moral core so solid that his level of honesty scared people. I remember him once finding a $20 bill and going up to the nearest person to ask if it was theirs.

I mentioned this about my father to auto- and moto-journalist Sam Moses in a conversation we were having about "cheating" and racing ethics. Sam replied, "So what you're saying is, your father's a chump?"

I'd like to think not, but maybe I'm a chump too. Also, maybe there's a context necessary: In everyday life? No. In racing? Well, maybe so. Thankfully my father wasn't involved in racing.

The hard and very, very cold reality of it is that racing ethics are not the same as everyday ethics. In racing, ethics are turned inside out and one is not a cheater if one doesn't get caught. Period. If you don't like that, don't race. But if you don't mind that, don't get me wrong. If you do get caught, you are a cheater and you have violated racing ethics. It's a difficult game.

The ethics of engine building for professional racing are perfectly encapsulated by the sentence: "This sentence is false." If that sentence is true, it's false, and if it's false, it's true. Or, if you prefer, if it's right, it's wrong, and if it's wrong, it's right. In other words, it's not proper to use the word "cheater" referring to those whose bikes are "outside the rules" but have passed through tech. If a bike doesn't get disqualified by the racing organization, then its crew did not cheat, end of story. Period. Everything else said about that engine is theory, speculation and gossip. Thinking you "know" someone has "cheated," even though they have passed through tech, is to know nothing. The fact is, the bike passed through tech and was officially declared legal, which makes it legal. No crybabies allowed.

My mistake was trying to make the team go AMA Supersport

racing with engines that would not only pass through tech but would also pass through the Pearly Gates. The thing is, the engines of most of the teams around us would also pass through tech but then go straight to hell. As they should because there's no place in any rule book that says an engine must pass an inspection by Saint Peter.

After flying home following a race, my father surprised me by being at the gate. Originally we had planned on him dropping me off at the airport and picking me up when I returned. But I had run late and had to drive myself to the airport and pay four days' worth of exorbitant parking fees. So it was very nice that my father had bothered meeting me anyway.

After we picked up my bags, he insisted on helping me carry what little luggage I had and then helped me load it into my car. Unfortunately, I had to leave for work directly and couldn't spend any extra time with him. So I drove to the parking-lot tollbooth and handed the attendant the parking stub that had sat on my car's console for four days. She scanned it through and said, "That will be $1.75."

I laughed and told her she was wrong and should look again. She did and then said, "That will be $1.75."

I laughed again and told her that couldn't possibly be correct. I told her my car had been parked there for four days and there must be something wrong with her computer.

Now she was getting perturbed as she repeated, "It's a $1.75," while holding out her hand. It was clear she was losing patience. I wasn't sure what to do and just sat there for a moment staring at her. She then suggested that maybe the guy who was in the car behind me laughing had something to do with my confusion. I thought, "What?!"

I looked in my rearview mirror and saw my father behind me laughing, and now waving a parking ticket in the air. The thieving bastard had stolen my parking ticket and replaced it with his!

Again I laughed, but now at my father's joke. I paid my $1.75 and drove off thinking about how funny this pretty crafty joke was that he had played on me. Then suddenly, a moment later, a feeling of horror and resentment washed over me.

My father had never doubted for a second that his son would do anything at that tollbooth other than protest being undercharged. And his son never thought of doing anything other than that. But I'd just learned new ethics that my father didn't know and wouldn't understand. He doesn't know racing. He doesn't know anything about not getting caught meaning it's not wrong. My new embrace of racing ethics could have polluted my thinking and made a simple loving joke of an innocent man inadvertently into a test of ethics. I could have done something my father hadn't anticipated, such as pay $1.75 as if it were my due, and broken his heart.

So I now know that I will be sure to never, ever slip and confuse racing with the rest of life. I'm happy being a chump and making a father proud. And as far as racing goes, I can, without equivocation, say that my team has never, ever cheated. Just ask any tech official. Period.

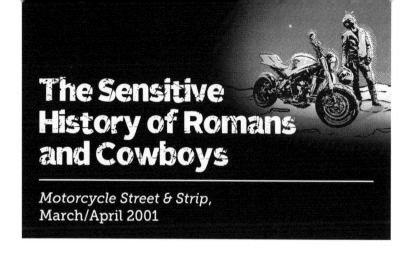

The Sensitive History of Romans and Cowboys

Motorcycle Street & Strip,
March/April 2001

Does your crotch hurt? Mine does. I don't mean my ass hurts, or my package. I mean my crotch hurts. That intimate area centrally located between, and maybe including, the business parts between my legs. You know, that soft area where the sun never shines.

It hurts because I was out riding a motorcycle. There's no reason to name which brand of motorcycle I was riding, because my crotch tends to hurt after riding most any brand of motorcycle. I am certain though that this doesn't happen because I have an unusually hypersensitive crotch. In fact, my crotch, probably like you think of yours, is only exactly as sensitive as I'd like it to be. So I'm betting that many of you suffer exactly as I do when riding a motorcycle. And I suspect you're suffering in silence, fearful that admissions of pain will be taken as admissions of weakness. But it's not you, or me, or us, it's the seats.

In case you're wondering if I have the proper credentials to talk professionally about crotches, yes I do. I've taken college courses about how to make seats that don't hurt crotches. I essentially have a degree in the proper design of products that don't hurt people; a degree in Industrial Design, which is the degree that professionals who design products have. During my studies, I had to learn big words like: ergonomics and derrière. That first one is the science of how humans interact with things designed for humans to interact with, such as seats. That last one is French for ass. It's likely you already knew that one.

My schooling taught me that our crotches become sore from motorcycle seats because the seats are designed so that we're unable to sit on what we are designed to sit on. And instead we're forced to sit on our crotches. Crotches aren't designed to be sat upon. Crotches are designed to be sensitive, which we appreciate when … well, you know.

The reason our crotches are between our legs is to keep them out of harm's way. But when riding a motorcycle we have little choice but to spread our legs and plant a too-hard and too-narrow seat up our butts, willingly allowing motorcycle companies to have their way with us intimately and rudely. There is little that's badder than sitting on your bladder, or your prostate. Sitting is what asses are for. It is why asses come with their own padding. It's why we have ass bones.

When I was a kid, I once took a very long bicycle ride and ended up with a blister on my crotch. It didn't leave a scar on my skin, but it certainly left one in my head. My recent crotch pain has reminded me of that horror. Also, as an adult a motorcycle ride from Iowa to New York state bruised my tailbone simply from sitting on a motorcycle for those many miles. OK, some of you might want to argue that a tailbone isn't actually located inside one's crotch. But since it's within the crotch's greater metropolitan area, and prone to seat-induced pain, just shut up.

Anyway, this contusion to my coccyx plagued me for six months. I could sit on it without suffering, but whenever I stood up from a chair a sharp pain shot up from my ass up through my spine. Often that pain shot upward so fast it would involuntarily shoot right out of my mouth. "Yeow!" I would involuntarily exclaim. As with a crotch, a tailbone is not meant to be sat on. It's susceptible to shock fractures and a number of valuable nerves pass around it. If those nerves are damaged, the consequences could be permanent.

Humans are designed to sit on their pelvises. The pelvis is that giant bone that connects the top of us to the bottom of us. The spine goes in the top end of it and the legs come out of the bottom. The word "pelvis" is derived from the Latin word for basin. That's because the pelvis is our basin; it cradles everything inside us and without it our stomachs and kidneys would be slapping against our thighs. So the pelvis is big and thick and strong, able to support the weight of our hanging guts, bodacious bosoms, double chins, fat heads, and whatever else we might have loaded up onto ourselves.

The human pelvis, like those of monkeys and every other animal that likes to sit on its ass, has two bones fused to its bottom called the ischium. Pronounced *iss-key-yum*, with the emphasis on "key." They are those big loops that hang down from the pelvis, inside of and below the sockets for our leg bones, which are connected to the knee bones, which are ....

Sorry. The ischium are designed specifically for sitting on, and they're not in our crotches. To find them on yourself, place a hand under the bottom of each side of your ass and sit down. They are the hard parts of your ass that are now crushing your fingers.

A couple hundred centuries' worth of lazy design students have given us chairs with broad, flat surfaces bigger than most human asses, causing us to think that flat chairs provide seating bliss. What they do provide is the chance to stuff a big pillow under ourselves and the ability to shuffle around. But wide seats and big pillows don't fit too well onto motorcycles. So, after long rides we tend to walk like cowboys. And of course, cowboys walk like Romans, who are the originators of crappy seats on things that move. Or was it the Greeks?

Despite this long shared history of suffering, the solution to fixing motorcycle seats is nothing new. I've read that it was the people of the Yunnan province of China who, centuries ago, invented a horse saddle without a center section. With that saddle, the crotch, the package, everything located between the legs, hung free while the saddle supported the rider completely and comfortably on his ischium. How this simple, intuitively obvious technology got lost, I'll never understand. I mean, it doesn't even involve a moving part.

Those of you who ride bicycles for sport have already noticed that the wisdom of these Chinese mountain people has been rediscovered. But the split saddle is still unavailable for motorcycles, with the exception of the ill-fated Bimota V-Due, which at least had that one thing right.

A Guy and His Bike

Motorcycle Street & Strip,
July/August 2001

A rider who works on his own bike has an idiot for a mechanic. Another racer and I created this cruel variant of that old adage about a lawyer who represents himself to describe a similar truth about how to be an idiot while road racing. There are great riders and great mechanics, but there are no great rider-mechanics. Being very good at one of those two things takes unique abilities and a severe dedication, both of which tend to preclude being exceptional at the other task. Each endeavor distracts from the other one's goals.

If you think about it for a moment, you'll realize the real cruelty of our paltry joke was against ourselves. We were attempting to pride ourselves on how our semi-failed racer-selves had been held back by our idiot mechanic-selves. The thing is, for both of us it might have actually been the other way around. Or, of course, it could have been we were held back by our broad reach of mediocrity in all projects.

Anyway, from knowing this about road racing, I've been assuming the same should hold true for drag racing. But now that I have spent some time at the drag strip, I can see the same truth does not apply.

The fascinating fact is that in drag racing nearly the exact opposite of road racing is true. A drag racer who works on his bike is often a winner and is also often a multitime champion. Many, many successful drag racers do much of their own tuning, if not their own complete engine building. Why is that? There are probably a number of reasons.

Road racing is primarily about the rider. It's a sport where the person in the saddle can make up for a few faults within a machine. But just a few. And, unlike in drag racing, every track is radically different. The only similarity is that they're all paved. Well, except for Nelson Ledges, which is made out of layers of crumb cake. Now I don't mean to say there isn't considerable skill, dedication and practice necessary to properly launch and race a drag bike and get it to the other end of a drag strip quickly. There is. But considering how many times a drag racer can screw up in 10 seconds or less, think of how much time a road racer gets to botch things up during a 15-lap race, with the possibility of losing time entering, apexing and exiting every turn on every lap. The opportunities for screwing up a lap are astronomical.

Drag racing, on the other hand, is mostly about the bike. If the bike has any fault, the rider loses. In drag racing, every track is the same length, the lights flash in the same timed sequence, and getting to the other end of one is pretty much the same as getting to the other end of any other. Sure, different tracks have different grooves and some have bumps. But still, the only variables, theoretically, are the rider and the bike. When a drag bike rider performs well, he succeeds in being like a machine, making the bike the only variable. And in a botched run, a drag racer feels as though he's let his bike down. The racer knows what the bike can do, so they know who to blame when that performance is not accomplished. Road racers, on the other hand, feel no allegiance to their motorcycle. And they generally have no shame in being quick to blame the bike.

Drag racing is also all about fast. Fast without distraction or compromise. Fast, not as an activity, but as a cultural quest. Braking late and carrying high cornering speeds are not about going fast, they're about dodging obstacles. The first rule of fast is to take the quickest way between two points. And don't screw around by jimmy-jamming the bike here and there and everywhere else. Turning scrubs off speed and is a nuisance. Don't waste time. Turn the throttle, press the nitrous button, and let 'er rip. Anything that causes a drag racer to lift, even for only an instant, is in violation of the goal of fast. Power is right. The more power the more righter. In drag racing, there is no such thing as too much power because there is also no such thing as turn one. There is, of course, unmanaged power.

Anyway, turns are wrong. Turns are stupid. Turns require the horror of having to slow down. And besides that, turns are dangerous. You can trust me on that one. Sure, drag racing has its risks. But they're all associated with the speed itself, not with braking contests like those occurring at the end of every straight on every road racing track. Although highly entertaining and requiring great skill, braking late is simply not about speed. Holding a throttle wide open is about speed.

A drag racer is often an engine builder. A drag racer is a motorhead. A road racer tends to find working on his bike a nasty distraction that interferes with preparing mentally to ride. Meanwhile, for drag racers, building and tuning a bike is preparing mentally to ride. Far from interfering with a drag racer, doing a tweak here and there on a drag bike is exactly how many drag racers get into the proper mental state for a run.

Drag racing's culture of speed, no matter how legitimized by drag strips, comes from the street where it's a social activity. Because of that, the street culture of the sport will never be left behind. Because of that, drag racing, even at its most professional, is more of a cultural experience than a sporting event. It's about a guy, or girl, and his and her bike. It's about the enthusiasm for the internal combustion engine. It's about grinding and polishing and modifying. It's about the smell of fuel, the feel of metal, and the bond between creator and creation. It's about the pure performance of power and acceleration.

By and large, professional road racers don't share this fundamental relationship with their machine because, essentially, they don't even have a motorcycle. They have to rely on borrowing one from a crew who are at a road racing event while often wondering why they're not drag racing.

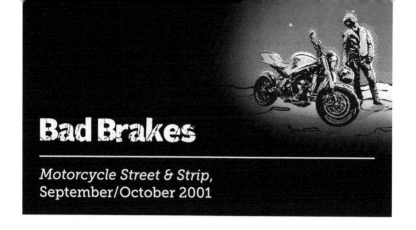

Bad Brakes

Motorcycle Street & Strip,
September/October 2001

Trying to explain motorcycle dynamics is like telling an elaborate and obvious lie; it sounds so stupidly implausible that you quickly lose your audience. This is because motorcycle dynamics are shrouded by a fog of intuitive bias that most riders tend to bring to the problem. Countersteering is counterintuitive. Well, actually, everything about how a motorcycle steers is counterintuitive.

Because of this, many bikers ride their motorcycle by applying control inputs they don't even know they're applying. They developed these skills as children on bicycles. And then as adults they have a muscle memory of what works and what doesn't, while having no intellectual knowledge of what works and what doesn't.

Early on in my motorcycle riding life, I inadvertently had an experience that taught me something about how motorcycles steer. I had taken the front brake rotors off my car to have them turned. But the only means for me to deliver them to a shop was on my motorcycle. This was complicated by not having any bungee cords or backpack. So I put the rotors in a cloth bag that had a shoulder strap, threw the strap over my right shoulder, and headed off on my motorcycle with the rotors hanging against my side. I'm guessing it was about 15 pounds of dead weight hanging from me. Of course this all seemed like a good idea at the time. What could possibly go wrong?

When I slowed for the stop sign at the end of my street, the bag slid down from my shoulder to my forearm where it swung side to side. I hadn't yet slowed very much, and the motion of the bag sliding down and pulling on my arm caused my motorcycle to veer quickly. I corrected for this and the bag swung back the other way, turning the bike hard in the same direction I was trying to correct it toward and causing me to wildly oversteer. I quickly pulled hard on the bars to correct for that while the bag swung back, causing me to wildly oversteer in that direction. I was suddenly trapped in a terrifying cycle of cause and effect and did not know how to get out of it.

This cycle of weaving and overcorrecting was self-accelerating. The weaving was becoming more and more exaggerated, which was causing the bag hanging from my arm to swing faster and further, which was causing my weaving to become more and more exaggerated, which was causing ....

I was trapped in a self-multiplying inertia machine of death that was quickly degrading into a "I-want-my-mommy" moment. My every attempt to correct the problem only exacerbated it. A bag of what should have been inert iron had become the dynamic steering force to my motorcycle, and I couldn't reason with it.

The weave soon turned into a wobble, which is to say, the rate of oscillation quickly and drastically increased. It was at that point that the bag of rotors was banging off the fork leg on its forward stroke and slamming off my leg on its rearward stroke, whipping back and forth harder and harder with the added energy of being sent back in the other direction by what it was crashing into. As the rate of oscillation increased, the believability of my survival correspondingly decreased. I was eventually slaloming toward a ditch with both of my feet dragging on the ground and cast iron bashing my thighs. (I do realize this whole event was a guy thing and basically another example of why the youth mortality rate is higher among males than females.)

Maybe it should have been obvious to me that I simply needed to let go of the bar with my right hand and let the bag of rotors fall to the ground. But I was in confused panic and inexperienced at what to do when riding a motorcycle with a weight hanging from my arm that was trying to kill me. Plus, it was my right arm that had the bag hanging from it. And since the front brake lever is on the right, I was operating on the assumption that hanging on to the bar might provide the ability to not crash.

I would like to convince you, and myself, that I am reliably heroic and brilliant. But I did not save myself by letting go of the right bar due to an inspired instant of problem solving under duress. I let go of the bar because the bag on my arm was swinging so wildly it tore my hand from the grip. The instant my right hand was off the bar, the bike stopped wobbling and straightened up. And as the rotors hit the pavement, I regrabbed the bar and braked to a quick stop.

Looking back at this incident, I'm glad I experienced it. It taught me something about motorcycle dynamics that I otherwise might not have learned, that "body steering," or swinging-iron-pendulum steering, is hugely effective if your hands are on the handlebars. Our shifting weight is transferred through our arms and into the bars whether we are aware of it or not. And, conversely, body steering without your hands on the bars is not steering. Sure, you can weave or veer when riding with no hands, but you can't actually go around a corner. It also taught me how dangerous cars are to motorcycles, even if it's just a couple minor parts of one.

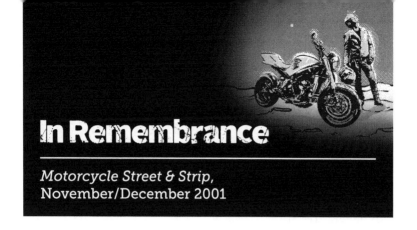

A ll of us at *Motorcycle Street & Strip* send our very, very deepest condolences to the families, friends and coworkers of the thousands of victims of the recent terrorist attacks. Our hearts are heavier than words can say and each of us grieves deeply for all of the loved ones lost or injured.

There are subjects appropriate and inappropriate for a motorcycle magazine, and the boundaries between them are usually clear. The job of such a magazine is to inform and entertain ardent enthusiasts about the sport of motorcycling. Anything that distracts from that is annoying ... at best. It must always be respected that, as a group, motorcycle enthusiasts may only have their enthusiasm for motorcycles as a common bond. But it is a strong bond, one that allows strangers to easily forget and forgive any other differences in their embrace of fellow cyclists. That is a big part of what makes being a motorcyclist so special.

With that understanding, due to the enormity of recent events, on this page we are stepping beyond our normal editorial boundaries. Choosing to do so was a difficult decision but, in this instance, not doing so would have been inappropriate.

It is impossible for us to go forward without taking a moment to express our condolences. It is impossible for us to produce this issue of the magazine without taking time to ponder the heinous events of September 11, 2001, in New York City, Washington, D.C., and rural western Pennsylvania. From those sites to all of America and across much of the world, millions have been deeply affected by these unprecedented acts of terrorism. The show of solidarity and support from people, countries and companies worldwide has helped greatly to reaffirm a belief in the solidarity of all mankind.

By chance, no one we know of who is directly involved in our niche of this sport was lost. But many were very close to where the incidents occurred and have lost many loved ones. At least one regular Prostar competitor worked in the World Trade Center. And our regular contributors, Tim Hailey and Matt Polito, both live and work in New York City and its surrounding area, as do many of you and others close to many of you.

Even though those of us who build this magazine were far from these acts of terrorism, we, like you, wherever you are, found getting through the days following the events greatly difficult. It has been hard for many people around the world to engage in activities beyond embracing the burden of empathizing with the pain and suffering of the thousands injured or killed.

As we prepared to send this issue to the printer at the end of the week following the acts of terrorism, it was still difficult to comprehend the scale of this event. Not just the scale of the immediate destruction and death, but also the scale of it to the human psyche and to our future. The world as we knew it on September 11, 2001, no longer exists. Those of us lucky enough not to lose anyone close to our hearts will still always find it easy to remember those taken on September 11, 2001, because our daily lives will forever be different.

Things we have learned to take for granted — freedom, security, liberty — are now redefined. It will be months, if not years, before we will fully comprehend the extent of the changes we will all experience.

Every man, woman and child of Flight 93 gave up the last minutes of their lives to save the lives of countless others. We grieve for and honor them. We also grieve for and honor those on the other flights and on the ground, whose lives were taken before they had a chance to show the sacrifices they would endure to save others. And we grieve for and honor the hundreds missing, killed and injured of New York's Finest and New York's Bravest. And we honor all those who have and are contributing to the rescue and recovery.

Godspeed all.

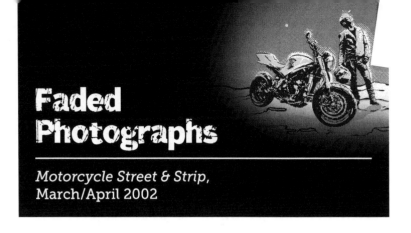

Faded Photographs

Motorcycle Street & Strip,
March/April 2002

I found an old pair of riding gloves the other day while cleaning out a bunch of boxes of "prized possessions" that I've had in storage for five years. They're slightly torn, the seams are loose, and they're covered in mildew. After finding them I toyed with them for a while, wavering back and forth between throwing them away or saving them.

I bought the gloves in Daytona during my first-ever visit to Bike Week in 1989. They're Frank Thomas gloves, made by a British company that seems to come and go from the U.S. market. At any rate, they don't import them to the States at this writing. The gloves are blue with red padding over the outside of the knuckles, long gauntlets, double leather in all the impact zones, and a field of metal rivets covering the heel of the palms. Thirteen years ago, they were the most beautiful gloves that I had ever seen.

I bought them at the Personal Cycle Center in Daytona. It was an Italian bike shop near one of the causeways leading across to the beach. They have long since gone out of business. I remember having admired the shop since they had all sorts of exotic bikes and hosted events during Bike Week for riders of Italian motorcycles.

That spring I went roadracing for the first time and wore

those gloves proudly and confidently. They were thicker than the secondhand ABC Leathers brand of leathers I wore, which had no double leather anywhere. A quality, brushed-cotton shirt is thicker than those leathers were. ABC Leathers has since gone out of business. I am betting they ran out of thin-skinned cows.

It rained on my second-ever race weekend, which was at Nelson Ledges in Ohio. I mention the rain before going into detail about that weekend just to be sure that my excuses are in order. Because I crashed. Twice.

The first time I crashed was entering turn one on the first lap. I had bogged the engine on the start because I was overly concerned with the driving rain that was soaking me and with the swirling colors of gasoline floating on the water around the bike, the result of an over-zealously filled fuel tank. I also botched it because I'd never been much of a street racer and launching a motorcycle from a dead stop wasn't a skill that I had yet developed. It wasn't a skill I had, particularly on wet pavement that had a frosting of fuel.

Having nearly stalled the bike on the start, I wanted to be sure to negotiate turn one like a pro. I remember grabbing the brake lever gingerly as I approached the corner. Unfortunately, my gingerly meter also hadn't yet been properly calibrated.

Sliding down the track on my stomach, it was incomprehensible to me what had just happened. Through my confusion of trying to figure out who had taken my motorcycle, I could hear the inexplicable sound of metal and plastic grinding on pavement. I probably slid a good 50 feet or more before I fully realized I had crashed. That was effectively 30 feet of utter confusion, followed by 20 feet of denial. I should probably add to that another 30 feet for the hindering fog of incomprehension to fully lift. In later reflection, the crash had reminded me of the time my brother Steve said he was going to punch me so hard I wouldn't know what hit me. He did. I didn't.

Fortunately, prior to this second racing event of mine, I had a local leather company stitch extra layers to the knees of the leathers over some aftermarket armor I had bought. The leather was torn through to the plastic, which was deeply gouged. I was deeply impressed.

By chance, the corner worker who happened to be working turn one that day was as good a corner worker as you'll ever find. He helped me pick up the bike and instructed me to follow him off the track while he pushed the bike. He told me to look over myself for damage while he looked over the bike. He needn't have bothered telling me that, because at that moment I didn't care crap about the bike. My hands were throbbing and the heel of one of the gloves was torn open.

I stood at the side of the track and carefully removed the gloves, making sure that none of my fingers came off with them. Surprisingly, all of my digits were still attached but my palms were purple and my hands were shaking uncontrollably. I was wet and bruised and frightened, and I wanted to go home and never race again. The corner worker then told me the bike looked ok and I was welcome to ride it around the track, back to the pits for a new tech inspection. I looked at him like he was nuts. I couldn't believe he could be so callous and eager to see me die. What'd I ever do to him?

Not wanting to tell him that I just wanted to go home, I put my wet Frank Thomas gloves back on and got on the bike. After returning to the pits and having the motorcycle re-teched to ensure it was not leaking oil or had any safety concerns, I found the nerve to re-enter the race. It was a two-hour regional endurance and all I was interested in was getting some track time. So going back out was still well worth the effort. Lord knows, I needed track time.

There was still a driving rain so I started out slowly, figuring that I'd behave myself and only go as fast as I felt I could safely ride. Each lap I found myself going a little faster until I eventually caught another rider who was, get this, going slower than me! After nearly the entire field passed us by, I went and did the unthinkable. I passed him, too. Oh man, I was starting to get the hang of this racing stuff, for sure.

I eventually came up behind another rider whom I was also obviously going faster than, but this rider wasn't going as slowly as the first guy. After a few laps I planned on taking him on the exit of the track's turn four, which I'd been warned was slippery on the outside. On exiting the turn I noticed that he was holding a really tight inside line, so I moved just to the outside of him, being careful not to venture out where it was slippery. The problem was, it was slippery everywhere except on that tight line.

The rear of my bike snapped out and I was once again sliding down the track. But this time, I knew I was crashing before I hit the ground. And this time, as I slid down the track, all I was thinking about was that as soon as I came to a stop I'd grab the bike and try again. Unfortunately, this time I'd ground through a side engine cover and my day was done. So were those gloves.

I'm saving them.

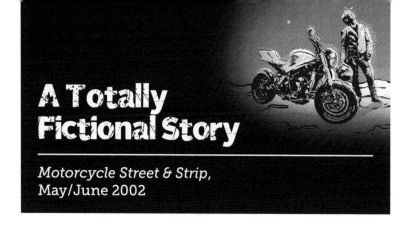

A Totally Fictional Story

Motorcycle Street & Strip,
May/June 2002

It's odd that we all drive vehicles capable of easily exceeding even the highest of legal speed limits in America. When the capabilities of today's motorcycles are considered regarding this, forget it. My main ride can break all speed laws in just first gear, and I have five more beyond that to play with. We're allowed to own vehicles that, with the tiniest of indiscretion, can lead to jail time. Buying a motorcycle today is sort of like being allowed to order a steak that you can look at, smell, pinch between your fingers, maybe even lick, but you're not allowed to actually eat it. (If you're a vegan, just replace the word "steak" with "broccoli.")

Because in my past I have been known to eat steak, a number of years ago I discovered the fine art of hiring a lawyer to "take care" of moving violations. Prior to that, I'd thrown myself on the mercy of the court. It doesn't take doing that more than once to learn that courts, generally speaking, don't have mercy. Judges are like physical therapists; they don't believe they're being effective unless you feel pain.

Once, when I didn't have enough money for a lawyer, I considered chancing the court's mercy. Waiting in the courtroom for my turn to plead guilty or not guilty, I figured I'd feel him out to try to determine the possibility of his charity. As I watched, a local farmer was called up to appear before him. This farmer also had a speeding ticket but not for a speed as egregious as mine. He explained to the judge how his family had lived in the local area for three generations, that this was the first speeding ticket he'd ever gotten in his 35 years of driving, and that he was very sorry and promised not to speed ever again, or at least another 35 years.

The judge replied that that was all fine and good but the farmer had to decide if he wanted to plead not guilty and have a lawyer represent him, or if he wanted to plead guilty and face the mercy of the court with the judge passing sentence. The farmer said he didn't know anything about lawyers, and so he'd just like to plead guilty and let the judge decide his fate. The judge said, "$250 fine, three points on your license, and the next time I see you I won't be as lenient."

The judge told him to pay the clerk and then he called me up to the stand. I screamed, "Not guilty!" and ran for the door.

The first lawyer I then called was young and virtuous. And she had a naive and confused concept of the law, thinking that it was synonymous with ethics. She asked me if I had, in fact, been speeding when I was ticketed. I admitted that, well, yes, of course I'd been speeding. She said she was sorry, but since I'd broken the law I needed to face the consequences and she couldn't do anything to help me.

?!

Well, if we lived in a perfect world, where ethics actually are welcome in the court of law, I'd likely have agreed with her and would have pleaded guilty. But if we're all going to tell the courts that we are guilty, what then is the point of lawyers? Isn't pleading not guilty automatically what you do when you are or are not guilty? Isn't the obfuscation of justice how lawyers earn their money? This well-meaning lawyer child, who'd somehow passed the Bar Exam, actually still believed that courts have something to do with right and wrong, fair and equitable, virtues and values, and ethics and truth. I called another lawyer.

Please don't condemn me for what I said above about courts of law not having much to do with ethics or right and wrong. It's not just my opinion; it's that of a lawyer. A real lawyer.

Anyway, another time back in the days when I used to go from one moving violation to the next, I noticed that I had a violation code written on my license: 1011. (This was back 1,000 years ago when a license was made of paper.) Knowing that I'd had a lawyer "take care" of a speeding ticket, I knew the violation wasn't speeding. But I didn't want to make a foolish claim in front of a judge that I was pure and law abiding while not knowing what violation 1011 meant. Maybe it meant burned-out taillight or loose rearview mirror?

I called the local sheriff's department and told them I had some mystery violation code on my license and couldn't remember ever having been convicted of anything. Crafty of me, huh? The sheriff asked for the code number and I told him, "1011." He replied that that code meant I'd gotten a ticket for some sort of moving violation and had hired a lawyer to "take care" of it for me.

Doh!

He went on to explain that in New York state there's no such violation code as 1011, so judges use that invalid code number when a lawyer has "arranged things." Whatever fine is assessed is sent off to the capitol offices of the DMV and rejected by the computer because there is no such code, and then the money is returned to that local municipality. By using this fictional code, municipalities are able to keep the funds from these fines in their pockets while judges statewide can share a record of whether or not you have a history of having moving violations "taken care" of.

I felt so … so violated.

It Happens

Motorcycle Street & Strip,
July/August 2002

Go crash your damn bike. I'm serious. If you've never crashed, you're either living in fear or living in denial. And is embracing either of those emotionally-defeating states any way to go through life? Um ... no. So come on, lay 'er down.

I don't have any close friends who ride without helmets. It's not because my friends are especially smart. What, are you kidding? My friends? No, it's because they've all used their helmets and so they know the reality of a helmet's value. They've crashed their damn bikes. Hell! Just like me, they've also crashed bikes that weren't even theirs. And they know they're going to do it again. Me too. Is the sky blue? I'll be crashing again.

The reason I bring this crashing and helmet stuff up is because a few days ago California legislators voted on repealing the helmet law. It wasn't successfully repealed. And too, *Motorcycle Street & Strip* has been in the center of the motorcycle-safety storm by (Me) running a number of stories with guys doing stunts on public streets without helmets. And, I also bring this up because a number of days ago I broke the pinky on my left foot when I clipped a chair leg while walking barefoot through my living room. Goddamn that hurt.

The impact of my toe against that wooden leg sounded like I'd crushed a bag of Doritos® with my fist. Convincing myself that the toe wasn't broken failed after one quick glance. That's because I'm certain it used to point forward in the same direction as my other toes, not out to the side at a sharp angle. Within a few hours, the broken pinky and the area below it turned a grape color. Not green, purple.

I tried yanking the toe back into place. But since I'm human, and humans have an involuntary aversion to causing themselves pain, l never quite got it back to where I'd like it to be. So I taped it to the other toes and there it sits. I'd like to say I've pretty well ignored it since then, but if that were true I wouldn't be writing about it now. What a baby I am.

Anyway, my toe? Helmets?

Once, while talking with a rider who hadn't been wearing a helmet, he explained that it was OK because he wasn't going to go over 60 mph. Hmmm ... I wonder how fast my foot was moving at the time of impact? I was walking at maybe 3 mph. I had to get that leg in front of me, so it was moving at 6 mph? 10? 15?

I asked this guy if he'd ever hit his head on something while walking and if that had hurt. He gave me a look that was so confused and vacant. Maybe I should have asked if he'd ever stubbed his toe. Stubbed his head?

Now, three days later, the purple has moved to my other toes and the pinky has turned yellow. ls that normal?

A helmetless rider in Ohio gave away the whole game to me. He told me he didn't need a helmet because there was no helmet law in his state. I asked him if the judicial laws of Ohio also had jurisdiction over the laws of physics. No helmet law, no need for a helmet, because there is no chance of possible injury. That's the kind of logic that transcends argument. That's the kind of logic that begs for there to be helmet laws. Because if there aren't such laws, there's no need to wear a helmet. That's how it plays out where there are no helmet laws.

The freedom of choice argument is effective propaganda, but it strays from the truth. The people who say they want to be able to choose do not actually want to make a choice. They simply do not want to wear a helmet. Period. They've already made up their mind. There is no choosing involved because if there was no law they wouldn't wear a helmet. So it's not about choice.

I also always thought that being a biker is supposed to be about being a rebel. Being a rebel is a cool thing to be, so everyone wants to be one. The problem is, few are willing to pay the price of the rebel lifestyle. But, duh, that's why being a rebel is cool and that's why everyone doesn't get to be one.

Being a rebel means that if you do not want to wear a helmet, you don't wear one. You don't care about no stinkin' laws. In fact, civil disobedience is what being a rebel in America is primarily all about. It's how our country was founded. We are the original laws-are-meant-to-be-broken nation. Plus, if there were no laws to break, it'd be impossible to be a rebel. That's what choice is all about. Choice takes guts, and freedom is just an excuse for being lazy. Like I said, just don't wear a helmet if you don't want to. Stickering up a crappy helmet is like beeping at a car that cut in front of you; it's nothing more than an announcement of losing. It's a display of helmet rage.

After five days, the discoloring of my foot has gone away but the toe is still swollen and is really sensitive to touch. Ouch! So I guess I shouldn't touch it.

Some laws do suck. Like right now, with my buggered-up toe, the California law that gives pedestrians the right-of-way over cars is stupid. Every time I get to an intersection while walking, the car driver that I meet there gets into an argument with me over who should go first. "No, you go." "No, you go." "No, you go." "No, you go." "No, you go." .... So I go and then they think I'm a jerk for walking so slowly across the street in front of them. To avoid this, I've resorted to acting like I didn't want to cross the street anyway. I'm just standing there bird-watching. "Wow, look, I think that's a pigeon. I'll have to put that in my journal when I get home."

Ouch! Maybe I should see a doctor?

The AMA fights helmet laws. [Not so much anymore.] So, in effect, the AMA promotes guys doing stunts without helmets. That's because guys ride bikes, and guys do wheelies. Girls do too. No rider is going to refrain from doing a harmless little wheelie simply because he's not wearing a helmet. And if there's no helmet law, there's no reason to wear one.

We report in here what's happening in the street, and we don't pretend that stunts aren't happening. And we don't pretend crashing doesn't happen either. It happens. It all happens.

So wear shoes.

We Are the Future We Believe

Motorcycle Street & Strip,
September/October 2002

here was a moment in my life when I had planned on drowning. I was 3 years old and an alleged family friend took me fishing in a rowboat. Although I had no fear of water and knew how to swim, my little orange life jacket was strapped to my chest as it should have been for a child on a lake.

The guy I was alone in the boat with was about 16 years old. He rowed us far out into the lake, the true distance of which I cannot now say as an adult years later. To my childhood brain it was a good 5 miles, though it could have actually been more like 1,000 feet. But all that matters is that, to me, as a child, it was very, very far. It was further than I had ever swum.

After fishing for a while, my host casually announced that the time had come for him to toss me into the lake. He reached over and started taking my life jacket off of me while telling me I wouldn't be needing it because the whole point of throwing me into the lake was for me to drown. I was numb with terror and didn't fight back, which seemed impossible anyway.

After my life jacket was removed, he sat back and asked me what I thought about being thrown in the lake. I don't remember if I responded. I do remember I was terrified and convinced that if he did toss me into the lake I certainly would drown. For whatever reason, he then said it was all a joke and handed me my life jacket. He then rowed us to shore while I tightly held onto my jacket and said nothing. I never went fishing with him again. I also made sure I was never again left alone with him on dry land. And, behaving just like most children, I never told my parents what had happened.

Something that fascinates me today about this event is how I had decided — even while still sitting dry in that boat — that it was absolutely impossible for me to swim to shore, and I was going to drown. I knew it as a fact that if he threw me in the water, I was going to drown. I think I made that decision because he expected it of me and because he was older than me, so he must have known the inevitable. I felt I had no choice but to die. So if he had tossed me into the water, I probably would have rolled into a little ball and sunk to the bottom without attempting a single defiant stroke.

Accidents happen, but oftentimes those involved are unwittingly compliant participants in their unhappy destiny. Someone recently e-mailed me a 10-second video of an amateur drag racer whose rear tire lights up at the line and steps out on him. The rider keeps the throttle on and simply drives off in this new errant direction to his left, crashing into the center divider and flipping over backward while taking out the tree. I must have watched the video about 80 times. I laugh each time just as hard as the first.

The video isn't funny because this guy biffs himself. Well … OK, that is funny. But funniest of all is how this rider gives himself up to being a victim. He could have let off the throttle, he could have turned into the slide, he could have jumped from the bike, or whatever. He could have done something. Anything. But no, he had decided that he was going to crash, that it was totally out of his control, and so he did.

This is also why I enjoy watching trials events. Most of what those guys do on motorcycles is exactly what we see in the moments prior to watching a normal human crash. Trials riders take what normal riders would consider precrash riding and ride it into more precrash riding while never actually crashing. Why is that? It is because they're not thinking about what they're doing. They're thinking about what is going to happen next, and so they always have a plan. They have a continuous belief in their ability to control their destiny. For any of them, a failed maneuver is simply cause for a new plan. They expect failed maneuvers. Part of this is simply having the tools of experience. But having those tools isn't enough. The other part is believing.

A car-racing instructor who familiarized me with the Formula Hayabusa race car we featured a couple of issues ago, warned the journalists participating that if the car's rear stepped out we should not try saving it because those cars were twitchy and snapped fast. He gave us an alternative plan, recommending that we turn with the spin, lock up the wheels, and hope for the best.

While then driving the car, I had it snap out on me in one particular turn. I followed my instincts instead of his instructions and saved it. My initial belief was that my actions had saved me simply by dumb luck. But on the next lap, I had it come out on me again. And once again I turned into it, lightly lifted my right foot, got back into the throttle, and again saved it.

In dealing with this problem, at first I found myself thinking it's best to keep the car from sliding, otherwise I'd certainly crash. The instructor told me I would. Then when I experienced the car,

I realized: Balderdash! The only reason for thinking I couldn't drive through a corner sideways was that I had been told that I couldn't. Now that I had information of actually doing it, I just did it. But now I also had something else: I had experience in anticipating what the car would do, allowing me to gain confidence in controlling the car. Crashing was no longer my plan. After that, I simply let the car speak to me, doing what it told me to do. Sliding the car was good.

It is in this way that victims can be made victims of their own minds, not of circumstances. Being convinced that destiny is out of your control is a self-fulfilling prophecy. And choosing what we believe makes us who we are. I know I am crashing a motorcycle when I feel the heat of pavement through my leathers. But up until that moment, I will rage against the machine. I will choose swimming.

Untold Tales of Bad Behavior

Untold Tale
Beware the Cloven-Hoofed Beast

How fast does this motorcycle go? During my first half-dozen years as a motojournalist, I had the professional duty of answering that question. To do so, I followed the industry standard of applying the scientific method: I would ride each new motorcycle as fast as it could possibly go while someone measured the speed with a properly calibrated radar gun. Or, sometimes I would hold the radar gun.

It was common in the late 20th century for moto magazines to do top-speed testing of new motorcycles on the high-desert highways of Antelope Valley, between the Sierra Pelona Mountains to the south and Willow Springs International Raceway to the north. The area is an ugly, arid, treeless expanse of sandy soil with highways running perpendicularly across it in a compassed grid. In those days, it was a place rarely used by traffic of innocent intent. It was where people go who don't want any witnesses of whatever they're doing. On a scale of seriousness of offenses, I'm pretty sure us motojournalists were amateurs.

We never wondered if top-speed testing motorcycles was a good or bad idea because it was crazy-ass fun, unnecessarily dangerous, generally illegal, and delightfully thrilling. So yeah, it encompassed all of the qualities that irreverent bad boy motorcyclists desire. I have even been top-speed testing with cheering manufacturer representatives, many of whom are bad boys that have corporate jobs. Good for them. Now that the days of top-speed testing are in the past, I'm not revealing any current secrets, just history.

In this area, the east-west roads are named by letters such as Avenue A, Avenue B and so on, while the existing north-south roads are numbered, as if one day this desert will be a city with all the missing streets filled in. It will one day, if the water holds out, despite the three-digit summer temperatures and blinding daily afternoon winds.

The north-south streets were preferred for the top-speed testing as they had few-to-no-one living on them, little traffic, and enough miles between intersections to reach top speeds on the motorcycles. Motorcycle magazines generally used only roads between 170th Street on the west and 110th Street on the east for maximum discretion. That area included about eight avenues.

At the zenith of top-speed testing in the late 1990s, it wasn't unusual for motorcycle magazines to run into each other on these high-desert highways — but not literally. The fight for ownership of certain roads between publications wasn't like surfers battling over possession of particular beaches and waves, which is a thing if you didn't know. We happily shared our streets of contravention, but we never shared our top-speed results.

On one of my early days of doing top-speed testing, we were on a street with barbed-wire fences running down each side and sheep grazing behind the fence on one side. On that day I operated the radar gun. As our rider returned toward me at full throttle in top gear on his first run, he and I finally noticed one sheep that was grazing on the street side of the fence. As the rider got closer, the sheep panicked suddenly running in full-out sheep gallop toward the road. By chance, the motorcycle was going fast enough that the sheep came up short of running in front of it. But it was sketchy.

After turning around, the rider pulled up next to me to discuss what to do next. I recommended that we leave. He said he didn't know what other avenues might be as desolate as this one, telling me he'd give it one more try while hoping the sheep would now be frozen in fear rather than frightened into flight. The odds were dubious, and the sheep wasn't talking.

On the next run, the sheep revealed it was already fully terrified in anticipation of the repeated threat of a high-speed motorcycle. By the time our rider was about a quarter-mile distant, the sheep darted at full speed into the nearest fence and bounced off landing on its side. Then it leapt up and ran across the avenue and into the fence on the far side, again bouncing to the ground. Once again it leapt up and headed back toward the road while giving a side wide eye to the bike closing in on it. The sheep then reversed course, darted back into the nearest fence, bounced off and sprinted back across the road at the almost perfectly timed worst instant, missing the motorcycle by inches as it passed by at a totally unreasonable, but for our purposes completely worthless, rate of speed. After that we gave up.

At a different publication, we did our top-speed testing on a street farther west. There was a house on that avenue, which made us nervous initially even though it was far back from the side of the road. One day while we were doing top-speed testing, the resident drove out to the road from this house and waved us over to his driveway. He told us he thought it was really cool that we had chosen the road in front of his house to do our high-speed runs. He also said he had a police scanner and would come out and honk his horn if he heard any concerning chatter. Not everyone hates motorcycles, even when they are ridden at high speed.

By taking motorcycles to their top-speed limits, we learned much more than how fast each motorcycle can go. It also let us experience how each bike behaved at high speed, which can differ greatly. Some bikes made high speed scary, some bikes were comfortable and well-planted. For instance, the Honda Blackbird would float at anything over 170 mph, while the Suzuki Hayabusa was just a lump of happy speed — 125, 150, 180 mph... there wasn't much difference. The 'Busa was always just super smooth and stable.

Top-speed testing also informed us about radar guns. We would begin the approach to the radar gun from two miles away to ensure each bike was fully topped out. Although the high desert is essentially flat, the bikes were out of sight two miles distant. So, we would squeeze the radar gun's trigger and wait for the numbers on the gun to start scrolling up, which always happened well before the motorcycle came into view. Generally, the motorcycles were at well over a displayed 100 mph before we could actually see them. This revealed to us that by the time a rider sees a police car parked on the side of the road, the officer inside has put the lid back on their coffee, hung up the phone call with their BFF, put their seat belt on, started the car, put the car in gear, and gotten bored waiting for one of our sorry asses to arrive. That's not to say that slowing down to show contrition is worthless. Just don't wave.

The era of top-speed testing came to an end when the manufacturers "agreed" to limit the top speed of their performance motorcycles. I will not testify about this in court, which is why I put the word "agreed" in quotation marks. Anyway, the agreed-to speed is 184 mph, but it only applies to motorcycles capable of otherwise exceeding 184 mph. It is a speed far beyond what most riders will ever try to reach. It's a speed that most states have no roads where there's enough room or privacy to reach. It is also a speed that's irrelevant to what a motorcycle speedometer might read due to a purposely built-in error of optimism. If your speedometer says you're going 200 mph, you're not. You're going maybe 184 mph. But you probably already know that from your GPS speedometer app and don't need any silly motojournalist to confirm it.

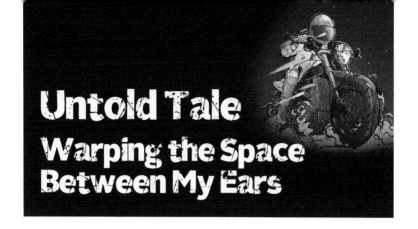

Untold Tale
Warping the Space Between My Ears

I walked into my first day at a full-time gig as a motojournalist like an excited purse dog, wagging my tail rapidly and nearly leaving a trail of pee on the carpet. I had been hired due to the chance vacancy of the entire editorial staff of a popular motorcycle magazine in the late 1990s. I had, at the same moment, vacated my position as Marketing Manager for a boutique motorcycle manufacturer. I was spending the winter jobless in Western New York. Spring came early.

Goodbye lake-effect snow and months of gray winter skies. Hello California. Surf's up. Hurray for me, I'm a journalist. I'm a freakin' motojournalist.

My office was on the 17th floor of a building on Wilshire Boulevard, about 800 feet east of Beverly Hills. My window faced the Hollywood Hills, providing me the classic you-have-arrived view of the Hollywood Sign. I spent my days there in the sky above the streets of West Los Angeles, writing stories about motorcycles, looking down on the people far below. In this scenario the ivory was a metaphor, but my tower was literal.

I rented an apartment a mere four blocks away, on the same block as the Flynt building. Yes, that Flynt; publisher of Hustler magazine. But the Flynt building quickly blended into the LA background, unable to compete with the daily weirdness of LA. For instance, within a few months of starting this job I had to use an alternate route on my walk to work due to an active armed robbery, hostage-taking, and shooting on Wilshire Boulevard. At work we watched the event unfold from the corner conference room on our floor. After the criminals were taken away, little yellow markers were splayed across the street and sidewalks marking evidence. There had been lots of gun play. California isn't just movie stars and surfboards.

The editors' offices on the 17th floor had windows, walls, and doors that could be closed (even locked), presumably so we could concentrate while authoring fantastic articles about motorcycling things. The central open cubical area housed the art directors, designers, copy editors and office machines. The Group Publisher and Editorial Director occupied two of the corner offices. The other two corners were separately occupied by a conference room and an exterior walkway around the HVAC workings, so we could actually go outside without leaving our floor. I think some people smoked cigarettes out there.

I noticed early on that few of the journalists, including myself, had ever actually taken a college-level course in journalism. The positive result of this was that none of us had the slightest concept of journalistic ethics. Even though that was disturbing, it was also convenient. I knew I would learn a great deal about writing, evaluating motorcycles, the culture of an industry, splitting lanes, etc., if I could survive this adventure emotionally, intellectually and morally.

I was also learning the culture of motorcycle publications. This was in the days of well-funded print publications with managing editors, copy editors, blueline proofs, and pages of draft copy passed around that would come back with corrections and critique from at least seven different-colored pencils. Each color was exclusively designated to a different reviewer, and each reviewer had different skin in the game. I was fortunate to work with two exceptional copy editors there, and one unexceptional one who seemed to think she was proofing grant proposals for a university. This "scholarly" one once had me read over a sentence I'd written that made no sense to her. After rereading it, I told her it was purposely an improper use of grammar for a joke that motorcycle enthusiasts would understand. She grabbed the page back from me, and as she walked out of my office door without looking back said, "Well, it's not funny."

In those days, there was a wise, old editor at one of the publications in our group who, when riding, always wore a 1990s vivid-orange helmet. Always. I mean, he never ever wore any other helmet. Ever. He also rode with good posture. Although I didn't much agree with his stoic dedication to unfashionable safety gear, he did have a well-seasoned sense of the motorcycle industry in that period of time. After seeing some of my writing, he shared with me that the real job of a motojournalist was to; "Just fill the spaces between the ads and don't cause any trouble."

That was a gut punch. It winded me. It undermined the irreverent fun I hoped to have and was the antithesis of my concept of being a motojournalist. I thought that words were supposed to matter. I thought that even though motorcycle magazines are enthusiast publications, there should be a moral basis to what is written.

Not surprisingly, I quickly failed him. Beyond that immediate failure, I can see that from end to end my motojournalism career has been a consistent failure at doing what he suggested. I am fine with this failure, though I admit his advice of pleasing the advertisers is sage business practice. It just isn't moral journalistic advice.

I also failed to adhere to his counsel when I wrote a review of an aftermarket company's website saying, "the graphics were cheesy." Mind you, this was in 1997 when few companies even had a website, including the manufacturers. For that reason alone, I should have praised the website.

The owner of this company called our office as soon as he saw the review. I wasn't in so he left a flaming message on my voice mail. On my return, I saw that my phone had melted. He called my boss, who also was unavailable, and left him a message of heartfelt anger. He then called the advertising manager of his account, chewing large chunks out of his ear. Following that, he faxed a letter to the publisher. He then mailed the same letter to the publisher through the U.S. Postal Service.

I called him back. I felt I owed that to him. He accused me of having a personal grudge against him. I didn't have a grudge. I asked him if I was supposed to only say nice things about everything. He said no, but I had gone too far. I talked with him until he seemed satisfied that I had gotten his message. At the end of the call I felt vindicated.

Looking back on this incident now, years later, I can easily see I was truly wrong. I was a naive neophyte journalist when I wrote that review. I was testing the medium. I had gone too far. But with that event, I learned how far is far enough and how far is too far.

OK, maybe I only have a slightly better idea today of what's proper and fair. No matter. I am fine admitting that I have often — maybe too often — failed as a motojournalist, if not causing trouble is the goal. But if my critical reviews pleased no one except the readers, I am fine with that even more so. I am still fine with that. I just no longer use the word "cheesy."

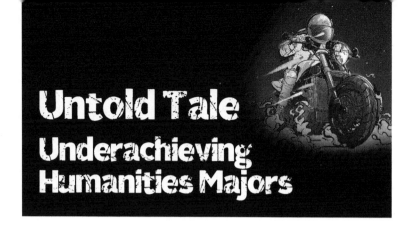

Untold Tale
Underachieving Humanities Majors

In my early days as a motojournalist, a manufacturer and a few aftermarket companies separately contacted me to discuss the relationship between them and the motorcycle media. They wanted to educate me on the symbiotic flea-picking grooming rules of borrowing motorcycles and acquiring accessories for editorial purposes. I quickly came to learn that there were specific reasons for my one-on-one schooling. Others before me hadn't cooperated.

A manufacturer invited me to its USA headquarters to discuss a loaner motorcycle that a publication had borrowed for use as a project bike for a feature story. The editors promised to return the bike after the project was completed and published. The manufacturer's representative told me that after a great deal of time elapsed without hearing updates about the project, they called the publication and asked about the bike's status. They couldn't get a solid answer. They continued contacting the publication, which continued to result in learning nothing substantive. Then the editors were suddenly no longer at that publication.

Diverting from that dead end, the manufacturer contacted the aftermarket shop where the project bike was being assembled.

This resulted only in more frustration. The manufacturer then notified the shop owner that a crew was on its way over to pick up the motorcycle.

It was at this point, midstory, that I was led into the manufacturer's warehouse and shown a motorcycle chassis and a few pieces of bodywork lying on the floor. I was told that this is what the shop gave them when they showed up to retrieve the loaned motorcycle. No engine, no swingarm, no fuel tank, no wiring harness, no fork legs, no wheels. It was a whole lot of not very many parts. I was pointedly told to not do that to any motorcycle company.

The racing manager of a major brand of tires invited me to lunch. He told me that magazine editors regularly ask for tires for testing motorcycles on racetracks, particularly when they are doing multibrand comparisons of motorcycles. This removes the tire variable in hopes that the bikes can be better compared, even-up, on the same rubber. He said this is part of doing business in the motorcycle industry and a price that a distinguished tire company knows they need to pay.

He then told me there was an editor racing in a national series who, without any discussion or agreement from this tire company, had decided that he was a fully sponsored rider on this brand of tires. At each racing event that editor would drop off his wheels at this brand's truck for free tires for practice, qualifying and racing, mountings included. The racing manager told me he could have refused to hand over free tires, but he feared doing so would have resulted in bad press for his brand. So, just because he was a motojournalist, that editor had a magical tire deal rivaling that of any factory team. The racing manager pointedly told me to not do that.

A motorcycle apparel company came to visit the editorial offices where I worked. Its representative told me how a couple of editors had squeezed his company for a new set of custom-made leathers for every project, for nearly every race event, and every multi-brand motorcycle comparison the publication had on its calendar. He said his company would love to have me in one of its racing suits for editorial features, even though they have a limited budget. He pointedly asked me to not seek, at his company's expense, a closet like Batman's with row upon row of immaculate custom suits.

SWAG, baby — Stolen Without A Gun — as a fellow motojournalist once defined it for me. That reminds me. If I ever get invited to an intro again, I need a new gear bag, which is always a great gift. And manufacturers please note: Do not put your branding on it. You know why.

Anyway, I was feeling a bit shy after these and other early meetings with companies in the motorcycle industry. I had yet to do anything wrong but I already felt guilty, which, of course, was the intention of these meetings.

It's a weird game of give-and-take in which much is hinted at but little can be spoken. Motorcycle publication exist through support from motorcycle manufacturers and aftermarket companies because these organizations buy nearly all the ads. But these magazines are also read by enthusiasts who want to be entertained while learning actual facts and honest opinions about motorcycles and products. It is also undefined what happens to aftermarket products after they are tested or reviewed. Rarely are they expected to be returned, yet it is frowned upon to sell them. Although I do know of one enterprising journalist who told me he made more than $20,000 on eBay in one year by selling every product handed to him. Don't get me wrong, that level of product does not normally change hands to any publication in one year. This journalist had aggressively shaken down companies for as much graft as possible. But at any level, as you can see, it's a relationship rife with complications.

The unspoken in this relationship exists because if an advertiser overtly agrees to buy an ad for a review of their product, they have purchased a review. And if a magazine tries selling an ad in trade for a review of a product, they have sold an editorial. And after it happens once that door can never again be closed. So, neither side is allowed to couch the relationship in explicit terms, while both are hoping the winks are noticed. Then along comes idiot editors like me who have no business sense and no issues about slamming advertisers' products.

This is why the salespeople are always better paid than the editorial staff. The first group makes a company money. The second group makes noise. The first group comprehends economics. The second group consists of undisciplined Humanities students for the most part; they're artsy yet ride motorcycles and drive vans. Motojournalists are why fathers have shotguns.

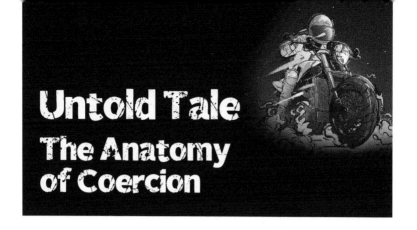

Untold Tale
The Anatomy of Coercion

The question enthusiasts most often ask motojournalists is: "What takes place at new-motorcycle introductions?" Well, I am not supposed to tell you.

But I will.

Within weeks of my new life as a motojournalist, my boss gave me a quick rundown of motoindustry practices at introductions, outlining the gifts (graft), global travel (sometimes graft), lodging (graft), and food and liquor (graft). I think he wanted me to be emotionally prepared before I was on an introduction so I would know how to behave properly, or possible misbehave properly. I am not sure which. He definitely wasn't giving me moral coaching.

As I would come to learn, motorcycle introductions of each brand generally adhere to the same basic practices, though they may vary widely in intensity. What I mean is, some introductions are primarily about a new motorcycle while others are basically festivals of marketing, better characterized as luxury vacations with parting gifts. One needs to be suspicious when pushed too hard with peripheral distractions.

The hosting manufacturer pays for motojournalists' travel to the introduction. The only exception is if the event is less than about 270 miles from Los Angeles. That means, if the event is in San Diego, CA or Las Vegas, NV, each publication has to fund its editor's travel or assign a freelancer and stick that yahoo with the travel costs. The USA West Coast introductions and brand events at the homes of manufacturers are the industry's way of telling publications that to be players in the game they need an editor, or handy freelancer, located where the action is: Southern California.

When attending international introductions overseas, I have at times boarded my first flight with $20 in my pocket, arriving back home three to five days later with that same $20 untouched. Usually though, I purchase some snacks and gifts and actually spend my own money for those things. The hosting manufacturer pays for the flight, all ground travel, food, lodging, liquor, entertainment, and maybe even days at a racetrack or the local police — if you know what I mean. Sometimes a few other entertaining diversions are paid for too. Flight quality can vary from First Class to Economy Class with a two-year-old child on the lap of the woman sitting beside you. For eight hours. That's not a happy experience, but life has few promises. With such possibilities though, Business or Economy Comfort seats are not really graft because a horrid international flight might not deliver a journalist in the right state of mind.

Whenever an overseas technical presentation for a new bike includes a local politician or chamber of commerce director, it means that riding like fleeing criminals on public highways will be forgiven. If it doesn't include such guests, be sure to have a few hundred dollars of American cash in your pocket. Cash dollars and a smile are the cost of forgiveness for traffic infractions in many countries. Strangely, some police in other countries do not ignore motojournalists' excessive speeds, running of stop signs, wheelies, stoppies, etc.

When I first learned that all expenses were paid by the manufacturers, I had ethical concerns. Any human should as it's a clear conflict of interest. But I knew I wasn't going to change an industry. I wondered though, just where is the line drawn between a critical review and a paid-for editorial? Can the graft be enjoyed while the joy of having graft is disavowed?

When beginning the journey to an intro, a few manufacturers have gone as far as sending limos to transport each journalist from their home to the airport. But that's rare. At the airport, if the journalists are flying out of Los Angeles, a representative or two from the manufacturer are there to be friendly uncles managing all things for the duration of the event. It's at that moment of meeting up with the brand's representative that journalists shut off their brains and any chance of responsible, adult decision-making. This is in fact encouraged by some brands, going as far as requiring journalists to hand over their passports to their new uncle for the duration of the trip.

At some point during an introduction a gift is proffered, usually with magical discretion. It might appear on one's hotel bed while out dining. Some gifts are reasonable, while some are far too expensive. Too expensive just makes everyone uncomfortable, breaking the spell of bad judgment. This can result in guilt, but not a lot of guilt. On the flip side, too cheap of a gift sends a negative message to motojournalists. At one intro we were given branded belt buckles. We asked if these were the pre-gift graft and were shocked to find out the belt buckle was all we were getting. Getting nothing would have been better.

The result of treating motojournalists like prima donnas is that they eventually become prima donnas, because being a prima donna is a fun thing to be. However, being a motojournalist prima donna is hard-earned and not just a free ride of fluffy happiness. For example, when arriving for a mountain ride and there is snow in the air, the journalists have to suck it up and ride without expressing a word of hesitancy. When arriving at a racetrack in a cold, driving rainstorm, the same applies. Without hesitation or complaint, motojournalists just get on the motorcycles and ride. It doesn't matter that there's nothing useful to be learned about a motorcycle from riding in 36-degree weather or driving rain on a racetrack on DOT tires. The manufacturer flew the journalists to a foreign country, rented a world-class racetrack, and provided the motorcycles. Ambulances are on-site and scratched bikes will be forgiven. Have a nice day.

Being a motojournalist is not actually a job, it's a lifestyle. Even so, some people are bad at it and it can become a grind. Like with everything in life, there can come a point when the joy of pleasurable friction evolves into painful blisters. That's when motojournalists need to keep their heads in place and stay the course, remembering that "real" jobs on planet Earth suck. After walking away from the castle of motojournalism, it can be impossible to get back in. I have witnessed some of the deserters desperately scratching at the outer castle walls after some time away. Few are given a second chance.

A serious downside of motojournalism is that the salary tends to suck — except for very few choice positions, most of which no longer exist. One journalist I worked with, when asking for a raise, was told by his boss to consider the graft he received from manufacturers as income. He was made to feel ungrateful for desiring monetary remuneration to clothe and feed his children.

Technically though, as far as the IRS is concerned, it might actually be true that those gifts are "income." The saving argument for journalists is that 99% of the graft is motorcycle-related and can be used in the act of being a motojournalist, making the items tax-deductible costs of doing business.

Most manufacturers are generally as behaved as possible within this conflicted culture. Some only participate within a moderate measure of graft just so they're not punished for not playing the game with the same rules. And they do it without handing out belt buckles.

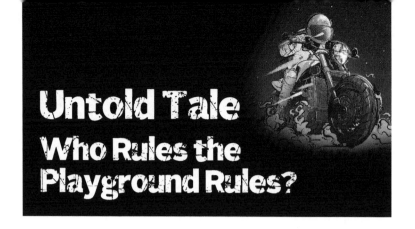

Untold Tale
Who Rules the Playground Rules?

A friend once told me that although two wrongs don't make a right, evening the score sure can feel good. It's about the worst advice I've ever received.

The motojournalist's lifestyle requires a fair amount of willful risk, bravado, and a desire to find the bleeding edge of things that go fast, make noise and can hurt you. Not surprisingly, self-regulated behavior is pretty much a rare trait in this profession. I mean, *motorcycles!* Is there not an onus of bad within that very word?

So generally speaking, motorcycle media events are like open-bar weddings featuring audacious episodes of gratuitous bacchanal hedonism. With the industry including motorcyclists on both sides of the editorial/manufacturer relationship — on both sides of the bar so to speak — sometimes it can get adversarial.

I was getting hints that one manufacturer was starting to perceive me as impetuous, unpredictable and dangerous. An early clue came when I showed up for a bike intro and was asked where my "friends" were. I asked, "Which friends?" There was a tone of disdain when I was told who my two special friends were. It was obvious there had been an intracorporate discussion about the three of us, as if we were a club. I shrugged it off and headed to the open bar.

This industry is a complicated mix of motorcycling culture, international corporations, rapscallions, old-school foreigners, economics, bad boys, manipulations, lies, dangers and risks in a fast-flowing, neck-deep river of conflicts of interest and man-eating predators. Oddly though, it's also a surprisingly conservative industry. No matter how hard I try, I keep forgetting that.

The uniqueness of the motoindustry is also complicated by the systemic burden of too many hardcore enthusiasts and a scant-few classically trained professionals merging at the same apex. Many upper-management corporate positions are held by individuals who started their careers on the sales floors of dealerships, not in MBA programs. On top of that, most of the motojournalists don't have degrees in journalism. But don't get me wrong — it just may be that for this industry people living their passions can result in an organic intuition no university degree can match.

Early on as a motojournalist, I was being pressured to conform to the established relationship between motomedia and motorcycle-related companies. There was pressure to author unearned and insupportable opinions that weren't mine. I needed to find a way to push back. It was wearing me out. When I finally devised a plan, it was ill-conceived. Worse yet, I would continuously execute it badly.

Sometimes taking the low road is just too much fun, even though it's poorly maintained and might not bring you to the destination you'd anticipated. Most of the manufacturers and aftermarket companies in this industry are well-behaved, which is a remarkable achievement considering they're all fighting for a slice of a limited economic pie. For the majority, self-respect is more valuable than dollars. But the bad one drags everyone down.

To prove I wasn't for sale to the misbehaving company that wanted to own me, my plan of resistance was to show it in return a mirrored level of disrespect, a carefully and thoughtfully regulated amount of disrespect. I should have predicted that the inherent weakness in my plan was my inability to properly moderate a level of discreet disrespect. I often misjudged, showing a bit too much disrespect.

As a witness to my life, I should have known that my natural tendency is to revolt against authority. I skipped classes. I dropped out of high school. I smoked cigarettes as a teenager. When I got my first driver's license, it already had points on it. So, with this intent of irreverence on top of my natural inclinations, it's not surprising that I might push back too hard. OK, I definitely pushed too hard. Fortunately, only one major manufacturer in the motoindustry suffered this resistance. In my mind they earned it. But in retrospect, I can admit an unbiased judgment might disagree.

But wait...wasn't my moral responsibility to be irreverent toward a pushy brand emboldening my journalistic obligations to motorcycle enthusiasts?

I'm not much of a drinker. For most of my life I typically haven't had a bottle of beer, wine or hard liquor in my home. Or if I have, I needed to dust it off when company was expected. This tends to make me a messy weakling when partying with the pros. Unfortunately, my propensity to hang out with hard partiers and ne'er-do-wells and ne'er do well with them had no aura of discretion about it. Once, at a domestic intro, my "friends" and

I showed up late at the track one morning after a night of hard partying. These ne'er-do-wellers and I figured the others would still be eating bagels and barely notice the lack of our presence. We were wrong. They were waiting for us before starting the motorcycle and track orientation.

That was the event at which my shove to their push established the game.

At a subsequent racetrack-based introduction, that same brand consultant waited for me to head out on the track and attached himself to the back of my bike as I exited pit lane. After two laps of wondering when he was going to ram me, I pitted. He did too, pulling up beside me. I told him to leave me alone and get off my ass. He said he just wanted to have fun riding along with me. What he really wanted to prove was that he was faster than me.

An introduction for this same brand's middleweight motorcycle was formatted as one-on-one rides taking place over the course of a week. On separate days, the manufacturer's representative led a journalist individually around the Santa Monica Mountains. This rider went far faster than any journalist I had ever ridden with in the mountains, and that includes many of the fastest of the fastest. It was immediately obvious we weren't testing the motorcycle, the manufacturer was testing us. So there was no way I was going to let this lead rider lose me or even drop me by two seconds. I rode tightly with him all day, committing to a pace I thought was inappropriate for public mountain roads.

After the ride, I called one of my fastest journalist friends who I knew relished trying to lose me in the mountains. He had been on this intro, so I wanted his opinion. He said it was a stupidly fast ride and agreed that its whole point was to be an angry test of journalists, not a test of a motorcycle. And this friend wasn't even a ne'er-do-well.

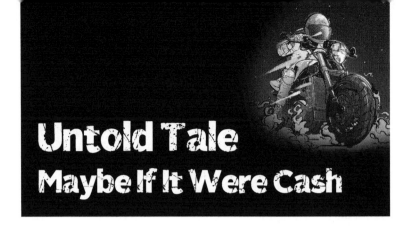

Untold Tale
Maybe If It Were Cash

I was disturbed by the culture of graft in the motorcycle industry, but what could I do? It's a matter of power and economics. It was ubiquitous. Basically, attending almost any industry function as a motojournalist involves being gifted something. I considered my options.

If I refused to attend introductions or corporate events, I'd be unable to do my job. If I refused the food and beverages and gifts at intros, I'd be blacklisted by manufacturers for being an unpredictable weirdo and fired for being unable to do my job. It was obvious I was not going to change the practices of an entire industry. No single journalist was going to change it. Few wanted to change it. Did I really want to change it?

Whenever an aftermarket company supplied me with gear or accessories for editorial purposes, I could have returned all of these items after the reviews were written. Have I? Who wants to know? Do I have situational ethics? Is that any of your business? Did I immediately get drunk on the power of being a motojournalist? Do I have to answer these questions?

On the day I justified to myself the selling out of my morals, I considered that somewhere beyond taking material gifts was a line

I would not cross. It was out there somewhere beyond the quarter-inch ratchet set, gear bags, backpacks, jewelry box, bike-washing supplies, clock, MP3 player (It's a crappy one.), watches, knives, gear, more watches, apparel and so on.

I wasn't the only motojournalist who was puzzled when receiving an invitation to a new-tire introduction that contained a crisp, new $20 bill. This mailed invitation was a limited-edition classy production of a folded, full-color, printed card created specifically for this event. The front of the card featured a life-size image of a pair of hands covered in grease. Inside the card, facing the $20 bill, it said something to the effect that the money was to grease the hands of attendees. Worse than the initial perception of this being an outright cash payment to attend a product introduction, the note inside came off as a purposeful insult to journalists. But clearly, $20 is not enough grease to be anything more than the bad joke it was most likely meant to be.

It's common for motojournalists to notice there is a great deal more money to be made on the marketing side than on the editorial side of this industry. So some leave editorial jobs to consult for manufacturers. The plus side of this is they understand journalists' needs. The negative side is they want to prove to journalists that they have mastered the game. So greasy hands and $20 arrive in the mail.

Within a few days of the $20 showing up, the tire company phoned every journalist who received the card and apologized. Apparently, the insult was a bit too much for even the old-guard editors, not just me. I accepted the apology. I did not send the $20 back, but I still have it if they want it.

I did, however, return the check for $500 I was gifted from a different company.

Not long after the $20 incident, I was assigned a trip to Spain for a tire intro of another brand of tires. This intro was an elite event, with only two American magazines invited. Shortly after this brand's agency was notified that I was an attendee, I received by mail my flight ticket and a check for $500. That was the moment I knew where the line was that I would not cross. Obviously, unlike $20, $500 is not an insult. It is far less than the amount necessary for me to give up what little moral code I might have, but it is not an insult. Well, OK, I guess it's a different kind of insult.

My boss saw it differently, telling me I was lucky to have been assigned an intro that included a $500 bonus. I grimaced internally. Then, without telling my boss, I mailed the check back to the agency that sent it.

The day after I mailed the check back, the proprietor of the agency by chance called to ask if everything was set for my trip. I responded that I was ready to go. I then added that I had mailed the check back. There was a long silence. He then said, "I hope you know why we sent you that check." I thought: Well yes, I do know why. His response seemed odd. We both knew why he sent the check, but we were not going to agree on the real reason. So I said, "Yes, I know why."

Even so, he felt the need to tell me the fictional reason why he sent the check. He said they wanted to make sure I had spending money while I was in Spain in case there was any reason for me to need money while I was there — for two days. While I was there being picked up at the airport, driven to the hotel the agency was paying for, eating the meals they supplied, being transported by them to the racetrack, spending a day riding motorcycles around the racetrack, and then returning to the United States the following morning after a second evening of comp'd boarding, food and wine. We both knew the reason why I had been sent the check. And it was the same reason, but not the one he suggested.

The other American journalist on this trip had only recently lucked into his position at a major motorcycle magazine. I considered telling him that I had sent my check back, but I didn't. I didn't want to embarrass, confuse or frighten him if he had pocketed the cash. As it turned out, about a month later he was no longer a motojournalist. At times, I have wondered if he disappeared from motojournalism because of that $500 check. Did he have a moral issue with it? Did he cash the check and his boss, unlike mine, saw that as crossing the foggy line?

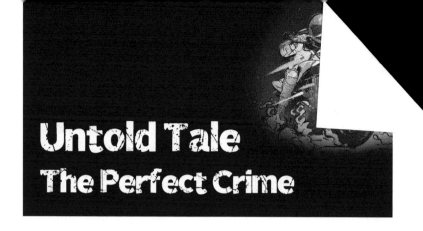

Untold Tale
The Perfect Crime

I generally prefer to stay out of jail. But I particularly prefer to stay out of jail in foreign countries. So, when the guard dog started barking, the French security guard started screaming, and the journalists scattered into the night, I was happy to have been witnessed beforehand as a nonparticipant.

Although new-bike introductions today tend to be well-behaved affairs, back around the turn of the century they were oftentimes a bit like international raves. An example of this type of motorcycle introduction that I attended took place in the south of France. It had a mix of North American and British journalists in the same wave, with a few scribes from other countries. I'd like to blame the Brits for the ongoing trash-talking competition between us back then, but that would just be me trash-talking. The war of words could have been their fault or our fault. Who knows? And there was an open bar. And...

On the third night of this introduction of a big-bore motorcycle, after we had completed riding the bike on the Circuit Paul Ricard racetrack and the highways around Le Castellet, France, we hit the partying hard. One of the American motojournalists had shown up for dinner that night with his name tag pinned to his shirt. A couple of us complimented his professionalism, as we had only worn our tags on the first night. This American was, by chance, a retired racer who is famous to some and infamous to others. No matter. In motorcycling both types of reputations are badges of pride, as proven by his induction into the AMA Motorcycle Hall of Fame.

After dining, the Brits and Americans congregated in the resort bar because we were trapped miles away from any other entertainment. After the brand's representatives from the attending countries headed to their rooms, someone suggested that we have a golf-cart race between the Brits and the Americans. The problem with that plan was it was late on a moonless night. The carts were not legally at our disposal. And, well, that demon alcohol might have been affecting judgment. Despite my compromised condition at that time, stealing golf carts just wasn't my type of bad behavior. Although I've never been much for obeying authority, I do not abuse other people's property.

The crowd shuffled outside toward the carts, which were parked in a row a couple hundred yards from the hotel patio, above the edge of a retaining wall facing the 18th green. One of my ne'er-do-well colleagues and I wandered out behind the others. We stopped to sit in chairs on the patio while the others continued on in the darkness toward the carts. After a few minutes, one of the American journalists came back saying he needed tools because the carts had locked ignitions. Shortly after he returned from the lobby with what looked like a tool kit, possibly nabbed from a motorcycle on display.

From where my colleague and I remained on the patio, we could only see general movements in the distant dark where the carts were parked. While we were looking into the shadows, a uniformed security guard walked up from behind us, heading toward the cart area. He was walking a large German Shepherd on a leash, even though we were in France. We greeted him loudly, saying how much we liked his giant dog and other ridiculous but friendly comments. We spoke louder and louder as if it were necessary for the guard to hear us as he walked on.

A few moments after the guard disappeared into the darkness, we noticed the shadow of someone shaking a golf cart violently from side to side until it went out of view. Then we heard a crashing sound. Immediately following that we heard the guard yelling, the dog barking, and numerous footsteps running on gravel. In the low light we faintly saw unknown figures running in various directions. We discussed what we should do, ultimately deciding that staying put was our best option for not being confused with the marauding miscreants.

Shortly, one by one journalists came running back past us, a couple of them with — literally — dirty hands. The French guard with his German dog came back by us moments later asking aloud, more to himself than us, "What kind of guests purposely destroy property? I am calling the police." We were impressed with his command of the English language. He then went into the lobby.

Having reestablished our innocence to the guard, my colleague and I figured it was time to retire to our rooms. Once we were in the lobby, we took to the open stairway that traversed four stories to where my room was located. As I neared the top, someone from above tossed a golf ball down those four stories to the lobby below. It bounced back up a couple of flights, and in between we could hear its loud raps from popping off floors and walls. And again we heard the guard yelling and the dog barking.

The next morning, we checked out of the hotel to be transported to Nice. As I was checking out, I noticed that on the counter next to me was the name tag belonging to that famous American racer. "Holy crap!" I thought. It was soon revealed to me that it had been found not just on the ground where the golf carts were parked, but next to a golf cart that was lying on its side on the 18th green.

About half of us Americans were now checked out, while the other half hadn't yet come down to the lobby, including the one whose name tag was on display. We sat silently trying not to smile or giggle. Eventually one of our hosts from the States said that because there were two vans transporting our group to Nice, those of us who were ready could leave immediately. We quickly fled for a van to avoid being trapped riding in the one that would be transporting the known hoodlum.

That evening, a journalist who rode in the second van shared details of the painful journey to Nice. We were told the Hall of Famer spent the two-hour ride rehearsing various versions of his story, hopelessly searching for one that might provide plausible deniability of his guilt. He reportedly failed to convince even himself. The predictability of him rehearsing an impossible alternate reality was why we had fled.

The publication that the name-tag-dropping, freelancing, former racer Hall-of-Famer represented was notified by the brand about what happened. That magazine cut its ties with him immediately.

At a later event hosted by this manufacturer in the States, one of our hosts on that France intro shared that the hotel had presented the brand with a bill for $6,000 for a wrecked cart, spilled oil, and a damaged 18th green. He said the American and British representatives agreed to split the bill, as they figured it was likely that both groups of journalists were involved. That sounded pretty reasonable to us.

Also during that later event, the manufacturer's host said he thought they shouldn't have told the publisher what had happened. He added that if it had been one of us regular-Joe loser journalists, sure. But this former racer, who is in the AMA Motorcycle Hall of Fame and is infamous for his irreverence and bad-boy habits, should have been given a pass. The few of us who had witnessed the event agreed. His reputation was well known so he shouldn't not be punished for being who he is.

That has long been my challenge — comprehending how bad my reputation can allow me to be, taking things only to where those who know me will simply say, "Well, that's Jones for ya." Too often I might have risked taking that challenge a step too far.

Untold Tale
The Dreaded Phone Call

When I was a foreign-car mechanic, my daily anxiety was the possibility of a returned repair. Each morning as I arrived at work, I'd scan the parking lot for a car that I'd worked on the day prior. Every now and then one would be there, silently mocking me. I'm an emotional guy. I take it personally when I don't do a good job.

As a motojournalist, my dread has centered around potential phone calls from pissed-off brands or insulted readers. Although this has been a monthly terror rather than daily, I have repeatedly promised myself to never ever again say anything critical about any motorcycle, accessory or society in general. But usually within a few days I'd always forget that promise and say something in the next issue that would piss off someone else. Apparently I can't help myself.

The manufacturer most infamous for such calls, however, has never called me. That manufacturer was well-known in the industry for grabbing journalists by the lapels at introductions and bloviating marketing hyperbole with spittle. At multibrand comparisons, that manufacturer would grill journalists on their developing opinions of each bike. And if the manufacturer felt like it wasn't winning the comparison, it would argue against the journalists' opinions. I almost have sympathy for the employees of this manufacturer, suspecting that they're either forced to drink laced sugar water or watch repeated showings of "Home Alone 2."

Now pondering why I hadn't received those calls, I guess it must be because the manufacturers had a hunch that, with me, the calls wouldn't be productive. Although I might be harshly critical, or even too critical, I am careful to make sure I know what I'm talking about. And I don't sway to marketing pressures. I think this brand's failed tests of in-person coercion with me put me on its no-call list. Also, I never say that any particular motorcycle is the worst bike ever or the best bike ever. There's no reason to name the worst or greatest motorcycle of all time before the end of time has occurred.

A manufacturer's media liaison once told me a certain motojournalist was no longer welcome at his brand's introductions because that journalist had said, in reference to one of the brand's bikes, "This is the worst handling motorcycle I have ever ridden." I acknowledged that saying that was improper, though I privately knew the bike was the worst handling motorcycle I had ever ridden. But there are other ways to express shortcomings without canceling a relationship. That said, since I am not mentioning brands, if that bike isn't the worst handling motorcycle of all time ever until the Earth is consumed by our swelling sun, I do not desire to experience the worst handling bike ever made.

Once though, a manufacturer did call me after my review appeared in print. It wasn't the brand manager who called, or the media liaison, or the product or marketing manager. No, it was the CEO who called. But the call was reasonable because English is not his native language, and his concern was caused by my odd misuse of my native tongue. The story's opener included a somewhat backward negative remark that was actually a positive comment about his motorcycle. My point was lost in translation, which should encourage me to write in a clearer voice, avoiding obfuscating terms and abstruse sentence structures. As if.

I explained to him the meaning of what I'd said, and he seemed satisfied though not thrilled. After we resolved that, I mentioned my impression of the motorcycle's rear suspension. But he quickly interrupted saying, "I know, I know, I know — we don't need to discuss that." Fair enough. He did know; it was on the pages in front of him. What wasn't on the pages in front of him was a story about how that motorcycle had caused me a minor injury.

All things considered, I was honored by that phone call. In the end, he had no contention with anything I had said about his motorcycle. He was not skeptical or dismissive of my impression. He wasn't angry or emotional. And he didn't question my ability to feel and comprehend the dynamics of a motorcycle. He only wanted to clear up some confusion due to my clumsy writing style. The problem with reviewing anything is that it's the same as criticizing someone's child. Even at the corporate level, emotions are involved. That's not just how it is, it's also how it should be.

Once I wrote a story about a pro racing series that earned me a letter from the racing manager of a different pro racing series. This letter was on his sanctioning body's letterhead. And it was purposely personally insulting, accusing me of yellow journalism, lying to the readers, and producing a biased editorial that read as if it were a paid-for advertorial. His accusations came off as odd since in the article hadn't once mentioned his racing organization. And prior to this, I had written quite a few separate pieces about his racing organization that were only positive. The meanness of his letter, received within the first few months of my motojournalism career, might have stuck with me a little too long.

Also early in my career, I made the mistake of offering the opinion in a motorcycle publication that the USA is a racist country. It was a neophyte error in which I'd forgotten that motorcycle magazines are supposed to be solely a source of entertainment for motorcycle enthusiasts, not investigative publications reporting on cultural issues beyond the world of two wheels. Shortly after that I received a voice mail from a reader who wanted to explain to me that the USA is *not* a racist country. He also felt the necessity to share with me that he was a Marine. Although I tend to call back people who want to yell at me, I didn't call him back. He called again, once again mentioning his rank and favored U.S. Armed Forces division. I still haven't called him back but I do try extra hard now to leave politics out of motorcycling.

Along these lines, in the days when stunt videos were ubiquitous, I was receiving piles of videos to review. Generally speaking, stunt riders were misbehaving motorcyclists who had figured out how to monetize their bad behavior. I finally gave in and watched one from beginning to end. It was terrible. Unfortunately for the stunt rider who sent the video to me, at that time my editorial irreverence just about matched the irreverence of stunt riders. I was purposely pushing the limit of what was acceptable in motorcycle magazines, such as featuring stunt riders not wearing helmets, performing wheelies and stoppies on public streets on the magazine's cover, and reporting about a street-racing event.

So, the review I wrote broke all the rules of polite decorum. I trashed the video in every way I could think of, going so far as to say the stunt riders were basically unlikable people. It makes me shudder in embarrassment to remember how caustic I had been. At a trade show where we were handing out that issue, the stunt rider who produced the reviewed video stopped by asking if he could take some copies of the issue to pass out to enthusiasts at his booth. We handed him a pile of them. As he walked away, I thought about how this might become an interesting day.

Untold Tale
The Fog Machine of Marketing

Reviewing motorcycles has become more and more difficult over the last couple of decades because the bikes in general are so damn good. Thankfully, there are still occasional duds.

I've written published pieces about the curse of damning with faint praise and the converse rule of etiquette to not use the word "suck," even when a bike might, well…suck. And I've seen a surprising number of my critical reviews lost in the noise of fluffy reviews from others. Still, one must try. Or maybe I'm just not doing my job properly of saying nice things about everything.

In the not-far-off past, I reviewed a bike that had a half-dozen concerning issues that I mentioned in my review. I later noticed that all other reviewers had raved about the bike. The publication I wrote the review for didn't give me another assignment for a year. This might have been intended to teach me something. Or was it just a coincidence? Could be. Anyway, when I asked the manufacturer about a number of the issues of that particular bike, its representatives were evasive. One suggested I wasn't riding the bike correctly.

As a rule, when at a new-bike introduction, I don't make changes to the motorcycle's suspension. This is because I accept what each manufacturer presents to us as its finished product. They ride the motorcycles prior to the events and make sure each motorcycle is set up correctly. So if they wanted the rear ride-height higher, they would have made it higher. However, if I am stumped by a new bike's uncomfortable handling after a day of riding it, I will sometimes give in to changing the settings to prove myself wrong. If I then prefer my settings, I have to figure out what that means. Thankfully this scenario is rare.

A few times though, in the last 20 years, there have been motorcycles with suspension dynamics that were exceptionally unbearable. At one publication we were loaned a performance liter bike for many days of evaluation. And we quickly determined it wouldn't steer with proper feedback. Two of us took it up into the Santa Monica Mountains where we would trade off riding it and an overweight, out-of-date middleweight motorcycle. I was initially riding the liter bike and my cohort the other. He was on my butt like cheese on a pizza. There was nothing I could do to get away from him. But I knew it was because of the bike I was riding, not due to my incompetent riding skills or his rare talent.

When we stopped, he laughed himself stupid, bragging about how he had just outridden me on a slow and heavy 600. I remained stoic. After we traded bikes I did the same to him, making sure I was consistently closer to him than he had been to me. When we pulled over this time, he was astonished by how bad that big-bore bike was. This is when we finally started making adjustments. But nothing we tried helped. It was just plain bad geometry. No knob can twist away bad geometry.

Another time I rode a new bike that wouldn't steer, it was at a racetrack introduction. That time the handling was to the point of terrifying. Once the bike was committed to a lean angle, it felt as though any attempt to alter the line through the turn would result in loss of control. The bike's front suspension was numb, providing zero feedback.

When a new motorcycle has issues, a manufacturer tends to already be aware of it and will try to market the flaws away. This is when one needs to keep their head above the swamp of qualifiers, lies, excuses and ambiguities. At one introduction, the motorcycle often popped out of third gear. And it soon became clear that a number of journalists were experiencing this issue. The manufacturer's pushback was to suggest that a media introduction is part of the development process, and this is how important the input from journalists is to manufacturers. It would have been fun for us to believe that. I mean, if not for our genius skills, that flaw may have gone unnoticed.

Something that always alerts one to the severity of a new motorcycle's issues is unanswered questions. "We will get back to you on that," is a telltale deflection of a real problem. In practice, companies do not get back to you on what they say they will get back to you on.

Although it's likely few to zero readers have noticed I don't mention any of the marketing materials manufacturers present to journalists at intros, there is often a considerable amount of it. Writing about the marketing efforts of a brand has always seemed to me like writing about what they have written about. Isn't the whole point to let each motorcycle speak for itself? Yet, when I get "too" critical, I then wonder if I need to remind myself that motorcycle magazines are entertainment publications for enthusiasts. We're not supposed to do investigative journalism.

I have had some publications I've written for ask me why I don't mention that I tested the bike on the southern coast of Spain, or on the Canary Islands, or that we were flown to the event in a vintage airplane or luxury helicopter, or stayed in a high-priced resort. While I'm trying to keep thoughts of being treated like a prima donna from influencing what I say about a motorcycle, telling readers about the princely treatment wouldn't help. But I wonder if readers take that to mean I am hiding something.

I guess that's why I am now sharing these stories. It's for fun, to entertain, to be transparent, to help enthusiasts have informed opinions before choosing to distrust me. Do not ever trust me.

I also wonder if any of this matters. I like motorcycles. Those who might read my reviews like motorcycles. Even a crappy motorcycle is great simply because it is a motorcycle. Riders tend to be brand loyal. So a bad review is often seen as unreasonable by those who love that brand. And for those who don't love that brand, it confirms their loyalty to another brand. There are likely few jobs in America less useful than that of a motojournalist. But it sure is fun.

OK, radio DJ is maybe less useful. Do they still exist?

Untold Tale
Catalonia Kerfuffle

A s a child, standing excitedly at an ice-cream truck with a teenager who resented the assignment of babysitting me, I modestly asked for a small chocolate cone. He changed my order to a kiddie cone. It was tiny. It was tiny compared to even my tiny hand. I was heartbroken. I loved ice cream. I swore I'd never put myself in a circumstance like that again.

At the last minute before leaving the USA for an international motorcycle introduction in Catalonia, Spain, it was announced that the USA manufacturer's host was unable to attend. In his place a lone underling was assigned the hosting duties. The problem with this was, as we would discover during the trip, this underling had unmanageable contempt for motojournalists and no intention of hiding it. Worse than that, it seemed his primary mission was to be all-in on his loathing to ensure that we'd be fully aware of it. From Los Angeles International Airport forward, the journey was an antagonistic game of one side biting the hand that feeds it with the other side biting the hand that pets it. We had to keep reminding ourselves that our host's unpleasant loathing of us was not supposed to be what we would be reviewing for publication.

From what our host said during that trip, the reason for his contempt was because motojournalists are prima donnas. I've no argument there, but that's not entirely our fault. Many corporations supply us with gifts, graft and adoration, and then aren't quite pleased with the outcome of entitled divas. The idea, for some brands, is to take advantage of our generally weak characters for better reviews. But our weak characters often miss the point and just seize on the joys of shiny objects. More please.

On our first night in Barcelona, the closest city to Circuit de Barcelona-Catalunya where we would ride, our host excused himself before we had a chance to order a single nightcap. This was unusual. Our expectations of free drinks for the prima donnas were dashed. So, we bought drinks with our own money and commiserated over how our first long day with our host had revealed his impatience, disgust, and dislike, in nearly every one of our interactions with him. We feared the trip might not improve. No ice cream for us.

The following morning, we piled into two vans. The lead van was piloted by our angry host, the second by me. The sky was threatening, but the air was dry. After following the first van for about 45 minutes, we noticed that we had come down many of the same streets two or three times and hadn't yet left the city. He finally stopped and admitted that he was lost, as if that was a mystery to us. Following countless attempts, we arrived at the track, after more driving in circles for over two hours. We later learned it should have taken us 28 minutes. As we arrived, the sky opened up with a drenching rain that didn't relent until late that night. Every journalist except us Americans had been on the bikes getting 90-minutes of dry track time.

We were at that point hating our host possibly more than he

was hating us. After a brief wait to see if the rain might clear, which it didn't, it was time for us to suck it up, suit up, and hit the track. So, we did.

There was a lot of scratched bodywork by the end of the day. I don't remember the final total, but it seems to have been about eight motojournalists hitting the pavement, myself and two other Americans included. It was just another day of riding in the rain on a racetrack on DOT tires. Our host was not pleased that a couple of us had brought cameras and taken pictures of the massive pile of bodywork in the dumpster behind the pit garages. Worse yet, some of us used those images in print

Yup, that dumpster appeared with my story. I should have known better. I did know better, but now suspect that it was my not-so subtle venting about our host's attitude. At least I hadn't let my review be influenced.

After my crash and checking out of the on-track medical center, I hurried back to pit lane for another motorcycle so I could try not crashing again. Waiting at our pit garage with a few other riders, our host from the States crashed a scooter in front of us. We involuntarily busted a laugh watching him slide by on his back. Yes, it was a heartless moment of schadenfreude. And guiltless too but heck, I've witnessed manufacturer reps laugh while watching journalists crash.

That night, our host abandoned us again. By this point, us journos agreed it was for the best. We wandered the streets of Barcelona, fought off a pickpocket, and had an angry Spanish drunk try to punch one of us because we were Americans. Initially he wanted to punch us for being British, but when one of us corrected him he settled for punching at his second-most-hated foreigners. It was a good night, all things considered.

This event was a two-day introduction, with the second day featuring a short street ride on dry pavement. That evening, our host took us to dinner in our hotel's restaurant and then once again deserted us. We were prepared this time, having surreptitiously gotten his room number for use at the hotel bar. We drank many toasts to his health, compassion, and gregarious attitude, and to our successful revenge.

On the bus ride to the airport the next day, our host mentioned that he noticed a significantly enhanced bill when checking out of the hotel. He said he would forgive our thievery rather than report us to our publishers or editorial bosses. For a few moments we liked him slightly more. Well, OK, for a few moments we disliked him slightly less.

Thinking later about why this marketing representative hated motojournalists so much, I figured he had forgotten that we were why he had a job. Plus, he should have seen that although we were a fun-loving bunch, we were appropriately professional when necessary. Work that requires an odd set of skills requires an odd type of human, no? I also knew he was infamous for his own bad behaviors. Back then, though, what I hadn't thought of was maybe he only hated a couple of us in particular, such as me.

He wouldn't come to like me any better.

A few years later, as Editor in Chief of a print magazine, I assigned a friend to an international introduction for this same brand. More than just a freelancer, this friend is a former AMA national road racing champion and has depths of personality. Lots and lots of personality. Once again, my angry nemesis was in charge of the intro.

Shortly after the introduction, my nemesis called me, asking if I'd spoken with my freelancer since the event. I told him we had chatted about when I needed his words and that was about it. He then told me that it was a two-day intro at a racetrack, and on the second day my freelancer didn't show up for transport to the track. He said they pounded loudly on his hotel door repeatedly and phoned numerous times without a response. They gave up and went to the track without him, not seeing him again until they met for dinner.

I apologized profusely, promising that that would never happen again. He said he wasn't going to punish my magazine in any way. He just wanted me to know what happened so I could be sure to control my contributors. I was surprised at his grace.

I called my friend and asked him if anything happened at the introduction that he might want to share with me. He guessed I had received a phone call. He said he was out partying late into the night with another journalist. He was passed out in his bed when it was time to get on the bus. He agreed he had let the magazine down.

It just might be that this manufacturer's rep was a better judge of us than I could admit.

Untold Tale
Cigarettes and Strippers

Sometimes, new-motorcycle introductions are symbiotic parties of shared indulgences between manufacturer and journalists. One such event for a Japanese brand took place in Rimini, Italy, where we stayed at a swanky historic hotel with a high-ceilinged, marble-floored lobby, ringed by Doric columns illuminated by the sun shining through walls of tall French doors. Located in the basement below this lobby was a strip club.

Italy is different from the USA.

Strip clubs aren't my thing. Not that there's necessarily anything wrong with them. Well okay, for me there are some things wrong with them. But this collection of stories is about bad behavior, not good behavior. And, when in Rome, or Rimini....

We had no idea there was a strip club below the hotel's lobby until our last night at the hotel. Following dinner and imbibing that night, our hosts led three of us journalists out of the hotel and around the back to a small, gated stairway leading down from a rear corner of the building. From my years of experience in the motorcycle industry, I've noticed that many Japanese businessmen still enjoy a culture of smoking and strippers. So do Eastern Europeans.

The club was so smoke-filled that I soon found myself bumming a cigarette to keep from choking on the used-up air. In the haze of smoke on both sides of my eyes, a classic American-movie Eastern European bouncer, with muscles on his face that alone could lift heavy objects, led us to our seats on adjoining couches. About six seconds after our butts hit the cushions, each of us were joined by our own personal stripper…I mean hostess. Like the bouncer, they too were from Eastern Europe. We knew this because they spoke English and told us so.

Eager to get to the business of relieving us of as much money as quickly as possible through aggressive persuasion, but not force, they all sat far too close to each of us and looked far too intently into our blurry eyes. The one who sat against me was majestic. She had giant eyes. She was over six-feet tall. She had great posture. She had manufactured blond hair. Before sitting down next to me she paused, looking down at me waiting for me to look up at her looking down at me. I looked up at her looking down at me. She sat against me, I considered sitting in her lap.

She was wearing an engagement ring. She had man hands. She was a company-town girl. But I couldn't tell if she was the company or the town. Sometimes, when you don't care if you're being used, it just doesn't matter.

Our bouncer friend showed up a few minutes later with a couple of bottles of the world's worst imitation champagne. The group was broken up and we were three journalists and a company rep sitting on couches around one table, each with a woman attached, though not necessarily voluntarily. The bouncer announced that the bottles cost the equivalent of $90 American. Each. He held out his hand for payment. Our American company rep paid. We were then told that in order for us to remain in the club there needed to be a drink in front of each of us. "Us" included our new friends. The women started gulping the sparkly down as quickly as possible. They were kindhearted and soon offered to help each of us empty our glasses. It was a pretty straightforward economic model.

As the night progressed, the women with us took turns excusing themselves one by one. Then each one showed up on a nearby stage to strip, which included taking off everything — except for, in Blondie's case, that engagement ring. After that, they each returned immediately to our table, clothed, as if they had just merely stepped away for a minute to get a pack of cigarettes or check their makeup.

When my long-legged blond went to the stage, it was obvious the other journalists, along with me, were particularly interested to watch her strip. Comparing notes with them later confirmed why. Like me, they were eager to know if she was a man or a woman. Don't get me wrong. She was beautiful and credibly feminine, but very tall and with a chin like The Rifleman. She had just the right amount of masculinity that for a heterosexual guy is equal parts frightening and seductive, which, of course, can be a good thing.

I had previously been told by an Italian that all of the good-looking prostitutes in Milan are men. I wondered, how far exactly are we from Milan? Maybe a couple hour's drive? I wasn't sure. I pictured her driving a Fiat Topolino, head down, lips pursed, a cigarette pinched between the first two fingers of her left hand, the spike of her right heel mashing the gas pedal to the floorboard, our two kids in the back seat crying, my right wrist handcuffed to the armrest....

She was a woman. Is. Well, who knows?

Our hosts eventually fled leaving us to sort out which of us were the victims and which were the predators in this club — us or them? Rasputin the Bouncer asked us if we were going to buy another bottle of sparkly vinegar. I said no. My cohorts said yes. For some reason it needed to go on my credit card. I figured it would help my Blue Angel save up enough cash to go get married. The sparkling beverage wasn't even good vinegar.

We closed the place, despite refusing all invitations to go to private rooms.

Maybe I should mention that on this trip we had been doing laps at the Misano racetrack, now formally named Misano World Circuit Marco Simoncelli. On this trip the circuit had not yet reversed direction and was mostly left-hand turns. It was a great bike that we were testing. Two wonderful days of riding.

I picture her doing laps in her Fiat....

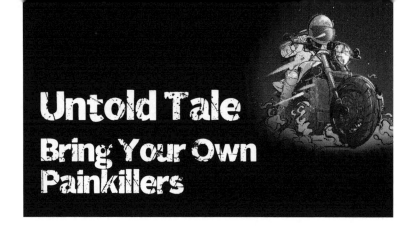

Untold Tale
Bring Your Own Painkillers

There are basically two types of motorcycle journalists: those who specialize in testing cruisers and everyone else. The first group are nice people. The second group…?

It wasn't until I went to the introduction for a cruiser motorcycle that I realized chest-beating, trash-talking, kill-switch-hitting motojournalists are those who test performance-type bikes, which is whatever you see on racetracks. Cruiser journalists are those who say, "It's a nice day, we're riding motorcycles. Life is good, peace brother." They smile, they lend each other a hand, they wait for whoever might be riding at a slower pace. They're weird.

So cruiser intros are basically chill events, except, of course, when they're invaded by a few performance motojournalists who are occasionally, accidentally assigned to those events. Not having a cruiser state of mind, they…I mean we, proceed to test the bikes through sweeping curves at 100 mph, howling the tires on braking and purposely grinding the floorboards on every curve. And yes, for some, wheelieing the beasts.

I've read in polls conducted by the Motorcycle Industry Council that maybe 2% of end users of cruiser motorcycles ride them aggressively. Heck, they don't even want to hear about the bikes they like being ridden hard by daredevil journalists.

Somehow, manufacturers generally show great patience while suffering these occasional circuses of wild monkeys wreaking havoc with the furniture. And then usually, exactly as they fear, the leading images in those published test rides feature sparks flying from the floorboards. Those reviews invariably mention instability at speeds over 100 mph, lack of feel during repeated hard braking, and, as always, complaints about cornering clearance.

I guess burning the chill out of cruiser intros is a cultural thing. Performance journalists just have an uncaged desire to win, even if it's not a contest and despite the manufacturers admonition that cruiser intros are not races. What? Many of us are former or current racers. So, go, go, go, kill, kill, kill, get out of my way, is a way of life. In the grocery store I push a shopping cart with that same exact attitude. "Lady, what's the mystery? They're Brussels sprouts. Just put them in your cart and move it."

Likewise, there is a bit of trash talk and competition between motorcycle publications that feature performance bikes. It likely began the instant there was more than one publication. Between publications, who is the fastest is the top criteria of the better-than-you hierarchy, with circulation coming a distant second place. Maybe when ad-sales people are bench racing, circulation numbers completely define the hierarchy.

Fortunately, it's only on rare occasions that rivalry between publications results in fisticuffs. Only once at an intro did I witness a fist flying in anger. There were fewer motorcycles than journalists at this event, which is a very, very bad idea. It's like being asked to share a candy bar. "Get your own." The one without a bike decided it was time for one with a bike to share. The journalist on the bike disagreed with the timing, so the other journalist punched him. Fortunately, with motojournalists it's always just in fun even when it's not. It took only a couple of years for the one throwing the punch to hire the one he punched. Rough love.

Because performance riders and those who have raced are experienced with crashing and breaking bones, motojournalists with that kind of background can seem cruel to normal people. But we would never make a normal person with a broken collarbone wait for three hours to be driven home just because we wanted to ride more laps around a track.

A manufacturer's media rep invited a few of us motojournalists to ride supermoto bikes at the kart track at Willow Springs International Raceway. This was an unofficial event tied into his brand's Superbike team renting the "big track," so the cost of an ambulance on-site was covered. Going into this though, we understood that although there was an ambulance on-site we were not actually allowed to use it. Using it would shut down the Superbike team's track time until another ambulance could arrive. Someone would have gotten fired over that.

Within maybe 10 minutes of us being on track, I watched as one of the other two journalists got so sideways coming off a corner there was no mystery to what would happen next. He chopped the throttle and launched off the bike toward the sky. This was followed by an unfortunate reckoning with planet Earth. He landed shoulder first. I couldn't hear his collarbone break, but I swear I could feel it. It was nasty.

While we helped him up, the media rep reminded us, "You all knew, of course, that although there is an ambulance here that doesn't mean that we are allowed to use it, right?"

Two of us journalists nodded. The one with the broken collarbone sort of said, "Arrrrrgh…" He was trying to be noncommittal, as if hoping the sentence he'd just heard was gibberish.

While helping this moaning journalist to a place to sit, we asked if he minded if we rode for a while longer before taking him back to Los Angeles — a mere 90 miles away — since we'd only been there for a few minutes and wanted to ride some more laps. He grimaced. That seemed like agreement to us. So, the manufacturer's rep and the two of us without broken bones rode around for maybe an hour or two…or more. However long it was, it didn't seem very long to us.

I'm mentioning this incident to put the other tales here into perspective. Making this journalist friend wait for us to have fun riding supermoto bikes while he was in pain from a broken collarbone isn't bad behavior to us. Broken collarbones are to motojournalists what skinned knees are to normal people. They're just an annoying possibility of daily life. I've broken mine twice. Anyway, once we left the track it was only a two-hour ride home. He whimpered every time the vehicle hit an irregularity in the road. We gave him some ibuprofen. He hasn't once held that day against us.

Untold Tale
The Morning After

There are times in life when it's best to stop for a moment and self-reflect. It's hard though when you're caught in the 100-mph inertia of wild times and deadlines. Nonetheless, my time to reflect was the morning after three of us motojournalists and one manufacturer representative were partying hard. Yes, we did have good relationships with some corporate personnel. Some of them are humans.

Our party was on a cabin-cruiser. We were smoking cigars, toasting life, and daring to actually unmoor the boat from the dock and pilot it out into the ocean. Somehow, even though it was late at night, we didn't experience the downside of a three-hour tour; we made it back to the marina. One of us did fall from the boat, though, but only after we returned to the dock. Well, OK, he was sort of tossed from the boat.

The journalist who fell had been standing on the edge of the boat holding onto a handrail. The factory rep started peeling away the journalist's fingers from the railing, in a sort of dare. The journalist then slipped, falling into the water between the boat and the dock, bouncing painfully off the boat. While pulled him from the water it was clear that he was hurting. Not surprisingly, he decided it was time to leave. Had he not been injured we might have more strongly encouraged him to stay.

The next morning, I reflected on how those two of my ne'er-do-well friends were taking the bad-behavior thing a bit further than where I was comfortable. I wondered if I might need to step away from them for a while to keep from becoming collateral damage. My plan of distancing myself from the motojournalist was canceled within only a week despite my intentions.

A manufacturer invited three of our group of bad boys to attend an introduction that, oddly, no other journalists would be attending. We were to be immediately flown up the Pacific coast to a regional airport, spend the night at an oceanfront resort, then ride the motorcycles unescorted back to Los Angeles. Of course, the three of us chosen by chance included this dangerous friend. Why was this even happening? What could I say? It was an offer I couldn't refuse.

Apparently, the three of us were invited to this exclusive introduction because the manufacturer had just completed a major introduction attended by many publications. After this event, fewer journalists than anticipated agreed to ride the test motorcycles back to Los Angeles. So, rather than ship all of the bikes they called us three to see if they could get more journalists on the bikes and ease their shipping needs. It was a peculiar conspiracy of chance.

Because we were flying into a regional airport on a small plane, we had to go to a tiny terminal at the Hollywood Burbank Airport. When I arrived, I learned my dangerous friend was afraid of flying and a hundred times more terrified of flying in a small, regional turboprop. So, he was throwing back drinks at the airport as fast as he could. This resulted in him loudly and profanely rambling on and on about every possible type of airplane disaster that was obviously going to befall us. Because he was making everyone within hearing distance nervous, a gate attendant told us that if we didn't shut him up we wouldn't be allowed to board the plane. We shut him up.

Once we were on the plane though, he started at it again, loudly predicting every crash scenario he could imagine, until a lone male passenger threatened him with violence. That resulted in the third one of us responding to this angered passenger with equal anger. Meanwhile, I was unsurprised about what a glorious day I was having and beginning to wonder exactly which of the horrid disaster scenarios he was fantasizing about would actually befall us.

We didn't die. We didn't even crash-land.

He sobered up in time for dinner.

At dinner we were treated to some particularly fine red wine. The bottle was huge. And somehow, when our hosts were later distracted, the treacherous one ordered another bottle. The server instantly disappeared. I remember sitting there thinking what happens next was going to be interesting. The server soon showed up again, but not with a bottle and a corkscrew. He showed up with a bottle that was already uncorked. Our host asked why it had been brought to our table. The server said it was ordered, as he filled a glass held out to him.

Dinner was over. The three of us motojournalists were suddenly alone with a giant bottle of wine. Our hosts had excused themselves for the evening and fled.

The next morning, while we waited for the dangerous one to appear for the ride, one of our hosts mentioned that my friend seemed to be a little out of control. I vaguely agreed with his concern.

When finally heading south along the coast on beautiful, curvy, California state Route 1, two of us noticed our fear-of-flying friend was having a difficult time keeping up with us. We stopped after a short while and asked him if everything was OK. He said he was just nervous about police, and he didn't want to get a speeding ticket. Because this was unlike him, it struck us as a bit odd. He usually rides the fastest and takes the most chances. He said he'd make a better effort to ride at our pace.

After another short while he was again out of sight behind us. We didn't want to ride for too long without him in sight in case there was an issue and he needed assistance. But when we again stopped to chat, he claimed he just didn't want to get a ticket. This time he shared that he had too many points on his license. We told him we'd try to ride a bit slower.

Even with our best efforts, we just couldn't maintain a pace slow enough to keep him in sight, enjoy the ride, and reach Los Angeles before nightfall. So on our next stop, we pressed him harder on why he was going so unreasonably slow. This time he finally came clean. He told us that on the night we had been partying hard on the boat, after he left us, he drove into a DUI checkpoint. He was in his underwear, soaking wet, and, as he confirmed for himself later, had three broken ribs. He failed the breathalyzer test. His license was suspended. So, if he was pulled over while riding with us, he would be headed to jail.

We berated him for not telling us immediately. We knew he couldn't let his boss or anyone in the industry know because he would be unable to test any motorcycles and lose his job. We told him we understood but torturing us without explanation wasn't a winning plan.

Unable to fix his problem and needing to beat a setting sun on a cool day, we bid him good luck and set off without him. He confirmed the next morning he had made it home safely, dry, and fully clothed. I had to wonder though: Were we dragging him down or was he dragging me, and maybe a couple other friends, down? Was he pushing harder than me at the edges to impress us?

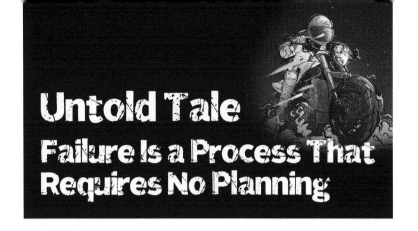

Untold Tale
Failure Is a Process That Requires No Planning

can't say it enough. I am not a fan of Las Vegas. It brings out the worst in people. It brings out the worst in me. So going there while having nothing good inside of me, would always be a particularly bad idea. A few weeks after 9/11 was not good timing for me to go to Vegas.

Because Vegas is Convention City, USA, and because much of the motoindustry is a convenient four-hour drive away (except on Fridays), many manufacturers host dealer shows and intros in Las Vegas. I've never been pleased about that, even on a good day.

I attended the motoindustry's first dealer show after 9/11. It was held just a few short weeks after 9/11, which I'm sure most would agree was too soon. All brands but one had canceled their September and October dealer shows. Was this brand being a brave leader?

Between 9/11 and this show, I had been working 12-hour days to meet the printer's deadline for a magazine that existed solely on paper. I was stressed out exactly like the rest of America; watching news religiously and fearing for the safety of grain silos in Iowa and other obvious targets of international terrorists. There was no means to emotionally deal with 9/11. It seemed as though reality was off its axis. It was difficult to comprehend what had happened even though we had all watched it live as it took hours to unfold.

By the time I finished that issue, I was emotionally burned out. I had nothing left. Nothing was funny anymore anywhere. The entire country was in shocked mourning. It took the late-night comedy shows a week to figure out what to do and when humor might again be funny. So by the time I was driving to Vegas, I reeked of anxiety. I'd had no chance to rest or destress since 9/11. Despite not being an avid drinker, I knew the instant I saw an uncorked bottle of wine I was going to surrender to its charms.

That evening, or whatever time it was in the city without clocks, at the open bar for the media meet-and-greet, I asked for a glass of red wine. Of course, without any urging necessary, I was handed a glass sporting a Las Vegas pour — low in class but topped off to the brim, baby.

When it came time for us to head into the brand's presentation to the dealers, we were invited to bring our drinks with us. I quickly had mine topped off. And as I turned to face the group on our way out, another journalist loudly exclaimed, "Wow Jones, that sure is a full glass of wine." The entire group turned and looked at me, including our hosts. I felt like I'd been involuntarily outed at an AA meeting.

After the presentations, we were joined for dinner by two of the brand's factory Superbike racers, and we enjoyed another opportunity to toast world peace. Following that, the racers and a few of us motojournalists (including my evil friend) headed to a bowling alley. It was around then that I felt as though I might have overdone my self-medication. However, one of the racers bought me a drink. It tasted like very sweet cherry juice. As a teenager, I wouldn't have consumed something if I didn't know exactly what it was. But apparently, I lacked all judgment by this point in the night and in my life. Plus, I was trying to be polite. This racer was famous, and I didn't want to insult him.

Then he bought me another one. I asked him what it was. He said, "It's good, just drink it."

I think the charm went out of the evening when I rolled one too many gutter balls and then ran after it to correct my error. I had no idea that the bowling alley lane beyond the foul line was like oiled ice. I also had no idea where my brain was. I hit the hardwood hard, giving up my mission and crawling on all fours back to the scorer's chair.

I quickly realized that the scoring screen wasn't responding to any of my inputs. I was about to ask one of the others what was wrong when I felt the weight of a firm hand on my left shoulder. It was a security officer. He informed me that our lane had been shut down. He said we were not permitted to cross the foul line under any circumstance and asked if I understood. I apologized and said I understood. He said he would have the lane turned back on and warned that the next time I do anything stupid there would be consequences. Even in my condition at that moment, I thought: Wow, only in Vegas. In any other city, police would have been involved.

The two Superbike racers suddenly decided to leave. Maybe I should say they quietly retreated into the night. I remained at the bowling alley for a while with my evil motojournalist friend and a friend he had brought along. Then we headed off for breakfast.

Back in the hosting casino, the three of us chose to sit in a circular booth and I was blocked into the back center of it. This became an issue because, by the time our food was served, I wasn't feeling well. I ate a couple of forkfuls then paused, setting my fork down. The room was spinning. A wave of hot sweat washed out from my forehead. A feeling of nausea rose up into my throat from below. I quickly announced to the two others that one of them needed to get out of my way immediately so I could run to a bathroom.

Still chewing, each of them turned toward me with looks of profound indifference. My evil friend then said, "We're in Vegas. Just stick your head under the table." He shoved another forkful of food into his mouth. I twisted around until I succeeded in getting my head completely below the table. My drinks, my dinner, my two tastes of breakfast, exploded from my mouth, spattering across the floor. Quickly I had nothing left to offer up. Rising back to a sitting position, I saw my companions were still chowing down their meals as if nothing unusual had happened.

I woke up the next morning in my room. I still had my wallet and my kidneys. I had again survived Vegas. Viva La Me.

Untold Tale
You'll Never Work in This Industry Again

Back to Las Vegas, the city of undoings. My "bad friends" did me in. Because of them I was blacklisted by a major manufacturer and I wasn't even present at the incident that prompted it. I was implicated by association. Well, anyway, that's what I believe and how I've told this tale privately for the last 19 years.

We were in Las Vegas for the racetrack introduction of a liter bike. After the first day of riding with two of my bad-boy friends— of course one of them was the same person I was trying to chill from—we again partied with intensity. Some might consider it excessive. Even so, at this event I arrived on time at the track for both days of riding.

Despite hating the town, I enjoy the road racing circuit of the Las Vegas Motor Speedway. It has a left-hand increasing-radius sweeping turn that leads out to the front of the track's trioval, which can be ridden at an ever-increasing speed to the top of third gear with a knee planted on the pavement. Reaching the trioval, the curve's widening arch is punctuated by a steep transition up onto the oval's banking that unsettles the bike. So I would get my knee off the pavement just prior to that. While riding street bikes through that curve, I had a habit of taking a quick glance at the speedometer just before the transition, once noting that 114 mph was my maximum speed there with a knee down. It was one of my favorite turns on a racetrack.

On the second morning of the event, my bad influence wasn't initially at the track. He missed the bus so he had to take a cab, joining us a short while later.

Although I had arrived on time to the track, my head felt slightly detached. Maybe I had too much to drink the night prior. Maybe I had stayed up too late. Maybe I had too much to drink too late into the night. Reaching the end of my first lap, while piloting the motorcycle through that high-speed turn and up onto the trioval banking, my actions seemed odd and hollow. The motorcycle's engine screaming toward redline, the speed, the wall of banking, my being there, it all seemed somehow incomprehensible and absurd. I wondered for a moment if I should pull into the paddock and chill for a few minutes. I decided no, I just needed a few more laps to feel the bike and the speed inside me. After those laps, I saw that I was right. I had adjusted to the strange dynamics of piloting a motorcycle at high speed.

After this second day at the track, the event had essentially concluded. But our hosts offered us another dinner and an additional night's stay at the hotel rather than forcing us to find our way home late in the day. I declined. My buddies of ill repute implored me to stay. They pointed out there was no downside to another free night in Vegas complemented by another free dinner and more free drinks. I headed back to Los Angeles.

Two days later, I was called by another motojournalist who asked if I'd heard that one of my buddies in crime had been fired and the other one might be fired also. No, I hadn't. I was told that following dinner on the night I returned to Los Angeles, my two friends were witnessed talking loudly and profanely. Apparently, the hosts had paid the bill and left the restaurant. But my two buddies were still at the table conversing, as were a few other journalists. One of those others called the hosting company the next day, relating the night's events and pointing out that the people around them must have known what corporation had been hosting this dinner that devolved into a Dionysian festival.

So calls from the manufacturer were then made to each of the publications where my friends worked. One motojournalist was fired by his publication without further consideration. This was because its Editor in Chief had emotional issues with this motojournalist and had long hoped for an excuse to fire him. The reason he had failed to pull the trigger sooner was because this journalist was the most popular editor at that magazine.

The manufacturer had a difficult time contacting the other journalist's boss because that publisher was in Thailand. When the publisher was finally contacted, the manufacturer was told the journalist was going to be disciplined appropriately—end of discussion. So the second editor was not fired. I have no reason to believe that my boss was called because he never mentioned anything to me. And as far as I saw things, there was nothing to discuss because I wasn't at that dinner.

About two weeks later, I learned through a fellow journalist that this same manufacturer was hosting an event at its headquarters within a few days. Normally I would have heard about this by way of an invitation from the manufacturer. Concerned, I called the media liaison at that manufacturer and asked about the event. I was told that there must have been an error causing my name to be omitted from the invitation list. He gave me the time and day I needed to show up for the event and apologized for the mix-up. But I wondered if something was afoot.

At the event, it felt a bit cool in the room. Even though the manufacturer had known ahead of time that I would be showing up, no effort was made to take care of minor hosting details, such as making a name tag for me like all of the other journalists were sporting.

This event was where I had first confirmation that my evil friend had avoided all consequences for his bad behavior. He hadn't been fired, he hadn't been blacklisted, and he was wearing a proper name tag. I asked him what his boss had said to the manufacturer. He said his boss basically told the manufacturer to deal with it. I had just learned another lesson in economics—his publication had many more readers than mine.

After the second or third time I was mysteriously left off the invitation list by this manufacturer, it was obvious I was blacklisted. Although no one inside the company would admit it. At least once the missing invitation was to ride a motorcycle. I called, and then I was scheduled a ride. So I decided I purposely wouldn't take the hint and I'd behave as if I hadn't been blacklisted, calling every time I heard they were having an event. And each time I ended up attending the event. If they were relying on me to facilitate this double-secret blacklisting, it wasn't going to happen. Maybe I'd shy up if they came clean on it.

Or…maybe not.

Untold Tale
Fake Love Lost

In my experience, hard work is rarely rewarded with success. Three motorcycle publications I was working hard for died ugly deaths on me—one crushed by its own too-rapid growth. I guess it suffered a form of deadly corporate gigantism.

During the time in between these failed publications, I was able to pick up freelance assignments from various motorcycle media outlets. Although this was fortunate for me, it was unfortunate for the brand that blacklisted me. I no longer had to rely on invitations from manufacturers to attend events, because I was now assigned to events by innocent third parties. Because that brand was hesitant to tell others I was blacklisted, it was left to suffer my presence. Maybe I wasn't washed up after all.

A print magazine invited me to be one of its team of test riders for a comparison of five middleweight motorcycles. As is the norm, the manufacturers involved in these comparisons attended the racetrack portion of the comparison. Some brands attend to monitor if there are any issues with the motorcycle they provided, while one brand is there to attempt to work over the journalists for a favorable review (as I might have mentioned in a previous tale). Of course that one brand is the one that blacklisted me.

Because there is no reason for a publication to announce in advance who the guest test riders are, two corporate representatives and the owner of their agency of record were unprepared to find me at this event. Their faces couldn't hide their displeasure of seeing me there, or maybe they meant to show it. There was a bit of tension in the air all day long but none of it was mine.

Despite my fall from their grace and their accompanying displeasure of engaging with me one-on-one, they still asked me during this comparison which motorcycle I was preferring over the others. Many motojournalists agree that this inappropriate grilling was most likely a corporate directive. We're convinced that after each comparison the reps are required to present documentation to upper management outlining which bike won and why. And it was always imperative for their brand to win. I imagined that reporting bad news to their corporate superiors probably yielded results similar to showing my report card to my mother.

Nonetheless, the day at the track went fairly smoothly and was followed by a dinner that evening for all of the participants. I don't remember why I showed up alone early, but I do remember that the air was chilly and I was wearing a faux-shearling coat. While waiting in front of the restaurant for the rest of the group, the three reps from my blacklisting brand arrived next.

As they walked by me to enter the building, one of them asked if I was a shepherd. I didn't respond. Then one of the others said that I looked more like someone who did more to sheep than just watch over them. I slowly turned my head and looked at them, wondering to myself if this type of engagement was a corporate directive.

As I've admitted, there was often a fair amount of imbibing

involved in incidents that contributed to me being blacklisted. The irony of that is in those years I rarely had any alcohol in my home and I only drank socially, which means drinking with others not drinking alone in public. Also, the one time I definitely pushed things too far was when I was under unusual stress and being supplied unsolicited alcohol by one of their factory riders. No matter, my behavior is mine.

Some years after being blacklisted, I learned one of the reps from that brand had told a person looking to hire me that it was hoped I would not be awarded the job. I was hired anyway.

Yet, in fairness to the manufacturer that blacklisted me, I've realized that even though I wasn't involved in the specific episode that was one-bad-act too many, I had been involved in enough other bad acts to earn being punished along with my cohorts who were at that infamous dinner. Plus, I was foolish to think I'd come out the winner in a battle of disrespect. All I had really succeeded in doing was to make them think I have a drinking problem. Playing a game I couldn't afford to lose was just a bad idea all around.

I was later assigned by another magazine to attend a large, annual, multiday event hosted by this brand. On the first day of the event there was a media meet and greet at a tavern. Immediately upon arrival, my faux-shearling critic welcomed me to the event. When we were quickly interrupted, he took the opportunity to get a beer for me even though I had not requested one. He returned holding it out to me saying, "I brought you a beer."

I told him, "No, thank you." Staring at me, he relaxed his reach for a moment and then pushed the beer out toward me again, saying, "Are you sure you don't want it?" I again refused. He asked, "Are you sure?"

At that point I just stared back at him. I was astounded that someone who thought I had a drinking problem was obstinately pressing me to drink alcohol. I wondered if he was being a free agent for his own amusement or following a directive.

This blacklisting lasted for a number of years, though I am unsure how many. Actually, I don't know if it ever officially ended or if it just sort of faded away following retirements, the hiring of new personnel, and failing memories. The company may still have a file on me. Although recently I attended one of this brand's introductions and there seemed, at the least, to be a truce in effect.

Untold Tale
Two Wrongs Make a Right

'**ve** learned the hard way that after years away from being a road racer, it's very easy to remember that I've raced and very difficult to remember how to race. That first type of memory only involves imagination. The second type requires engagement with the external world, muscle memory, proprioceptive feedback, kinesthesia, all sorts of other physiological interactions, and the suppression of terror. That last item might be the most difficult for an aging person to manage.

I achieved learning this the hard way in my last motorcycle road race, which ended with a crash on the first lap. Shockingly, the crash happened in an easy turn that didn't require much in the way of lean angle. Fortunately, having forgotten how to be fast, I was near the back of the grid when I crashed. Unfortunately, I still managed to cause one other racer to crash. His injuries were significant, but thankfully he is still with us.

I was taking part in this race by invitation from a team with factory support. One means of promoting the series was to put motojournalists on the motorcycles.

Two days prior to my crash, while out on my first practice lap, I leaned into the tightest turn on the track and the motorcycle literally would not turn. I don't mean the bike was awkward in how it cornered. I mean the fork pivoted slightly then locked in place. I could neither round the curve nor bring the bike back up straight. All I could manage was a wide, arching turn that the bike was locked into. I ran off the track into the grass and fell over.

Inspecting the motorcycle after I had righted it, I discovered the steering damper had not been tightened properly onto one of the fork legs and it twisted out of position binding the movement of the fork and causing me to crash. I walked the motorcycle back to the paddock where I showed the mechanic the problem.

While out on my first lap of practice the next day, I approached one of the hardest braking points on the track and discovered I had no brakes. I pulled back on the front brake lever and it went straight to the handgrip with zero resistance. I frantically pumped the lever as fast as I could but still had no braking power. Fortunately I was headed into a turn that had a paved escape route due to it being an alternative track configuration, blocked only by widely spaced hay bales.

After negotiating through the hay bales, I brought the motorcycle to a stop easily in the liberal amount of track I then had at my disposal. After getting off the bike and looking to determine why I had no front brakes, I saw that the two front brake calipers were dangling in the air attached to the motorcycle only by their flexible brake lines. The mechanic attending to the bike had forgotten to tighten the caliper bolts.

I didn't immediately find an obvious cause for my crash in the race, like I had with the two issues I experienced during my practice laps. It didn't make sense that the rear of the bike would snap out around me like it did while I was barely leaned over. Thinking back on the two incidents I encountered earlier that weekend, I then realized why I had crashed. When new tires are mounted by the tire supplier they have about 90 PSI in them, which is the pressure needed to seat the tires onto the rims. Every team is responsible to then set the pressures in their own tires at the recommended PSIs posted by the tire company. My neophyte mechanic didn't know this. I was trying to race on tires with three times the recommended pressure.

In my subsequent story about this event, I mentioned the steering damper coming loose and the brake calipers falling from their mounts. How could I not? I didn't bother mentioning the tire pressures. While preparing that story for publication, I received a bill for the crash damage from the owner of the racebike. I was shocked and incensed to be billed for damages when I truly wasn't responsible. Stewing over it, I still hadn't paid the bill by the time my story hit the newsstands.

A few days after that issue went on sale, I was called and berated by the team's owner for having written a story about this racing event even though I had only participated in the race for editorial purposes. He also said that minutes earlier he received a letter from the factory he represented notifying him that the contract between them was canceled due to the incompetency revealed in my story. He was squarely blaming me for his misfortune. I knew, though, that the factory cutting him loose had been in a state of flux and was looking for an opportunity to break this contract. I wasn't happy being used as the excuse for that contract being canceled. I felt used and abused by both sides.

I didn't pay the bill.

By coincidence, at this same time we had another model of

that company's motorcycles in my magazine's stable of test bikes. Returning from a photo shoot with our photographer piloting that bike, I watched him pull up into a wheelie next to me a few blocks short of us reaching our offices. As he motored out in front of me on one wheel, I thought to myself, "He looks dangerously too vertical." An instant later he and the motorcycle rolled further backward landing upside down on the pavement, with both of them then skittering down the street.

I pulled over next to the crashed motorcycle as the photographer jumped up and ran to it. We picked the bike up, quickly checked it over to determine if it was rideable, made certain that the $10,000 worth of photo equipment in his backpack was secure, and left the scene with haste. Back at the office my coworker apologized to me repeatedly, fearing that we would have to pay for the damages and suffer the ire of the publisher. I suggested to him that the brand should, in fairness, know that we were due forgiveness for this.

The next morning I called the brand's media manager and apologized for crashing one of his motorcycles, resulting in a fair amount of superficial damage. He quickly responded that he would forgive the damages and asked us to return the motorcycle as soon as we could. I thanked him graciously. The next time I saw that media manager in person, he shared with me that the CEO of his company had told him they can't just forgive magazines for damaging its motorcycles. He said he acknowledged the CEO's concerns but told him that this magazine needed to get a pass on this crash, no questions asked. We both silently knew why. I thanked him again.

Untold Tale
The Streets of LA

Early on in my career as a motojournalist, I suggested to the editor of the magazine I was working for that we should do a photo shoot of one of the new performance motorcycles in an urban setting. I was tired of all the photo shoots taking place at the same old racetrack and mountain roads. He refused, telling me that performance bikes always need to be photographed in their element: canyons. I suggested that Boston, Chicago, New Orleans, Miami, Indianapolis, and so on, don't have any canyons. He didn't care.

So when I was in a position to make such choices, I created a niche magazine for America's performance-motorcycle riders who aren't blessed with curvy mountain roads in their neighborhood. I referred to it as an urban performance magazine. At about the same time, a publication in the same niche titled Cycle Dreams appeared from New York City. It had a more robust ethnic slant than the magazine I created, as I didn't have cultural background to do that. Anyway, for a time this niche became a thing and a few other publishers copied the idea.

What I dug the most about my creation was that it put me in the streets with actual motorcycle enthusiasts, away from the high tower of motojournalism. The magazine's issues regularly featured urban bike clubs, female riders, custom performance bikes, stunt riding, bike club events, and other such things that frightened much of the motorcycle industry. I found myself with some riders and club members on rides that were basically raves on motorcycles. The day my new life led to attending a party for smoking green behind a house in Inglewood, California, I knew I had ventured from the approved path of motojournalism.

The bike clubs I'm referring to were not "outlaw chopper" clubs, they were urban sportbike clubs. A few of them were female clubs. Many of these clubs had events to which other clubs were invited. The urban bike club thing going on at that time wasn't about protecting turf or highlighting exclusivity, it was about inclusion. One of the major clubs in Los Angeles invited me to be an honorary member. I had to refuse so that I could remain neutral among all of the clubs. I was about to do a story on a bike club located in East LA, but unfortunately the magazine died before I could finalize it. When meeting with one of the club members in preparation for interviews, I was told there were certain questions I could not ask any of the members. I understood. This motoadventure opened Los Angeles up to me, and I hungered to embrace the city as widely as I could.

I butted heads with the publisher who preferred the magazine to feature fewer controversial stories. The stunt rider features also weren't impressing the manufacturers. So I was told to tone those down and no longer use images of stunt riders not wearing helmets. This made it impossible to feature many of them. So I asked the art director to draw helmets on the stunt riders, but do it in a way that looks like a child drew the helmets to let readers know we were being humorous.

The stunt riders we did that to did not see it as humorous.

Hanging with real motorcycle enthusiasts also led me to experience what it's like to have a police helicopter show up to contain these group gatherings. It's an unpleasant experience characterized by an overwhelming feeling of claustrophobia. There is no escaping a helicopter. Plus, as soon as you see one coming it's a solid bet there are police units on the ground headed toward you too.

At this particular gathering, two patrol units quickly showed up, with one of the officers immediately yelling, "Who did these burnouts?" The street before us was covered with donuts drawn in black rubber. The motorcycle I had brought, borrowed from a manufacturer, was the only one there with a scarred and hot rear tire. I feared I was about to lose the motorcycle.

Then one of the officers pointed at one of us and asked why he looked familiar. That rider, who moments earlier had been doing burnouts on the bike I'd brought, told the police he is a professional stunt rider and he had dropped off a box of his videos a week ago at the police station for them to enjoy. These police officers had watched those videos and in a crazy instant we went from criminals to celebrities.

The officers said they loved those stunt videos and apologized for bothering us. They added that they had a responsibility to respond to someone's complaint about motorcycles racing up and down the street. They asked us to please find a place that's more private to do our thing. Thankfully, we already had all the photos we needed and called it a day.

The one time I tried to attend a street race, the event was

canceled. It was an annual event that took place just outside of beautiful Fresno, California, in the San Joaquin Valley, which is a little more than 200 miles north of Los Angeles. I showed up at the secret location, but there was too much police activity so we were given an alternative address. The second location was a narrow, paved lane along a plowed field. There were motorcycles parked along both sides of the road, but it was determined that the police were watching so again nothing happened. It was a four-hour round trip to nothing.

One of my friends from the streets of LA told me how he avoided earning traffic violations. He said the trick is abandoning the motorcycle. Sometimes he goes to East LA first because the police don't like to go there. Or he goes into mall parking garages, abandons his motorcycle, trashes his helmet, then walks to the far end of the mall and has someone pick him up to take him home. The next morning he calls the police and reports that his motorcycle was stolen. I didn't ask him how many times he can do that each month before it's noticed that his motorcycle is very popular among thieves.

Thankfully, I had no interest in learning how to evade police.

Untold Tale
A Beautiful Spring Day

Eleven miles and seven police cars later, there I was, kneeling on a gravel road with my hands cuffed behind my back. The indignity hurt, but the pain of the handcuffs cutting into my wrists hurt worse. Neither of those pains, though, could compare to the trauma of a complete loss of freedom.

Moments earlier I was as free as only a motorcyclist knows freedom; face first against the wind in low acrobatic flight along a mountain road. It was a warm early-April day of my first spring in North Carolina. So, one of my brothers and I were out on my first-ever spring ride along the Blue Ridge Parkway (BRP), heading south toward Mount Pisgah from Asheville, North Carolina.

I had no intention of strafing the BRP at speed, but I also had no interest in spending my day stuck behind a white pickup truck going 10 mph below the speed limit. Complicating matters were six motorcycles between us and the truck. This caravan of seven vehicles was too long to safely pass in any of the very few passing zones. On the West Coast, slower drivers share the road and use turnouts to let traffic by. In the South, the culture of the highway is to impede others for as long as possible, despite the BRP having innumerable convenient turnouts. Because I wasn't alone, I behaved myself for 17.5 miles. I am sure some of you can empathize how difficult that was for me.

Finally, rounding a curve, I saw there was an open view of a long stretch of road without oncoming traffic. I grabbed the opportunity and passed all seven vehicles, staying on the throttle to give my brother room if he was going to also make the pass. Midway through the next curve a state trooper went by me in a Crown Vic headed in the opposite direction. I felt I had slowed enough before he came into view, but I wasn't sure.

I hadn't realized we were less than a mile from our planned exit, which I then took, rolling down the ramp and stopping behind a car at the intersection. The car pulled forward, turning left, the same direction I was about to go. I pulled up to the intersection and stopped again. I looked both ways and then started pulling into the intersection when I realized the car in front of me had suddenly come to a stop. While fighting to balance the bike and trying to figure out what the car in front of me was going to do next, I caught a quick glimpse in my left mirror of that white pickup truck coming fast down the ramp behind me. I've had bad incidents in North Carolina with drivers who hate motorcycles, and I was guessing this was the pissed-off driver I had just passed on the BRP. Because of that, and foolishly being halfway out into the intersection, I let the clutch back out, motored around the stopped car, and set off down the mountain at a brisk but reasonable speed. My experience has also been that if you take just semiaggressive measures to ride away from angry drivers, they tend to give up pretty quickly.

Within about a mile, I came upon another car. We were both nearing the entry to a left-hand, switchback curve so I was slowing. But as I closed up on the car, it slowed unexpectedly to nearly a stop. I grabbed an extra handful of brake and even though I was concentrating on this car in front of me, I caught another glance of that white pickup behind me in one of my mirrors. I was surprised to see how aggressively its driver was trying to catch me. Now even more concerned for my safety than I was earlier, I rode around the car, around the switchback, and then looked to my left up through the leafless trees to see for the first time that this wasn't the white pickup I had passed—it was a North Carolina Park Ranger SUV with graphics on its side.

F#@&%$*#@....K!!

I rolled off the throttle. I was being chased by a park ranger who thought I had been evading him for a couple of miles. A few weeks earlier I had an incident with a village sheriff who was only looking for trouble. I wondered, if I slowed now what would this ranger do—ram me, thinking that was necessary? Just last fall, that very scenario went down between a motorcyclist and a local sheriff. On a motorcycle I continuously make an effort to maintain control of the situation, hoping to increase my chances of avoiding injury or death. I was alone in the woods with an officer who might have tunnel vision, an excited heart rate, and an angry attitude. So I wasn't going to bet my life on his professionalism. Needing to make a quick decision, I chose life, promising myself I would stop as soon as another officer showed up.

I leaned forward and rolled on the throttle hard.

The first curve I came to I entered too fast and had to trail brake deeply into it. I told myself that if I couldn't relax and stop riding like an idiot then I needed to stop. By the time I came to the next curve, I had myself under control and was from then on simply blasting down a mountain road with plenty in reserve. After a few miles, I spotted pedestrians in the distance at a national park site. I slowed to the speed limit, thinking to myself that I make a pretty crappy criminal. After I was clear of that congestion, I wound the bike back up to my previous pace.

Upon fleeing, I knew this road had very few intersections and that they were all dead ends or loops. So I knew I had to stick to my plan of stopping. It was a long ride before I found another officer, and I hadn't anticipated that he too might be out of control. We crossed paths in a tight right-hand curve, and it was obvious he was driving at high speed...for no reason. Even at our approaching speeds, I saw his eyes jump open wide as he inadvertently jerked his steering wheel in surprise of finding me. I was suddenly stressed again, concerned that I hadn't found a cool-headed officer but rather one who had wound himself up on an unnecessary high-speed race to find me on a highway with limited options.

A few turns later brought me past a popular roadside waterfall with several pedestrians milling about. I again slowed, wishing I had time to figure out a new plan. Just past the waterfall was a road to my right that I knew was paved for only a short distance, leading to a gravel road that was often gated. I turned right. There was a trailhead parking lot immediately on my right, but again there were groups of people around. My concern was also that I didn't want to be arrested with an audience. I rode past the parking area and discovered where the pavement ended the gravel road was open, so I continued on. A few turns later, though, I had finished arguing with myself. I had no intention of running from the police; I was only trying to keep myself safe. So I needed to calm down and stop.

I pulled over to the side of the road, got off the bike, and removed my jacket. I was overheated and panting. I stood there for a while, still with my helmet on, thinking of different possible narratives of what to do next. I didn't like any of them, convinced that stopping and waiting for an officer was the best plan. It took longer than I had hoped, but the one who just passed me on the highway finally showed up. He got out of his vehicle and while standing at a distance, ordered me to lie face down on the road with my hands behind my back. He then came over and kneeled on my back, tightly clamping a pair of handcuffs onto my wrists. After he backed away from me, I asked if I could get up onto my knees. He allowed that.

And there I was, kneeling on a gravel road with my hands cuffed behind my back. He then told me that we were going to stay exactly as we were until the arresting officer shows up. I asked him if he could remove my helmet, which he did.

I was kneeling there cuffed, disrespected as a human, feeling like a trapped animal. I was a trapped animal. My autonomy suddenly didn't exist. Waking in the morning, making coffee, visiting family, turning on a lamp, gazing across a sun-washed field, twisting the throttle of a speeding motorcycle…all of that was suddenly out of my reach. If all people could be divided into only two categories, I think the two categories would be those who are by some means shackled, and those walking free. The shackled have no choices, plans or privacy, just a tainted hope. Life for the accused is a borrowed life; the person living it no longer owns it. It totally ruins a warm spring day.

After a short while, another ranger pulled in behind the first officer. Then a state trooper showed up and told me the best thing to do was say nothing. The problem was, I had already said, "He never used his siren." I said that purposely to show I was not shirking responsibility for what I had done. At no point had I desired to escape a speeding violation; I only wanted to keep myself safe.

Three sheriffs with mustaches showed up in three different vehicles. They were openly excited and pumped up from their drives there. Apparently, I'd been an excuse for a fair amount of unnecessary high-speed driving in the county that day. One of the sheriffs asked the ranger who I was fleeing from. The ranger filled him in. The sheriff then said that no one gets away from that ranger. I had to resist pointing out two errors in what he had just said: I had voluntarily stopped, and the arresting officer was still nowhere in sight.

Another ranger showed up, and after that it was a long while before the arresting officer finally arrived. I'd been on my knees for a good half hour. He walked over to me and looked me up and down, then said, "Yeah, I think that's him." I was surprised at his uncertainty, but that no longer mattered.

The rangers moved away from me for a discussion. Then the arresting officer came back and explained that this had evolved into something far more than a speeding violation, and I was being arrested for felony evasion on top of a few misdemeanors. He said the motorcycle would be impounded and he was going to transport me to the Buncombe County Detention Facility in the next county, because the county we were in did not have a jail approved for federal prisoners. That was a whole lot of words in one sentence about things I never thought I'd be associated with.

The motorcycle was a loaner that belonged to a manufacturer. So I was extremely concerned about whether or not it would ever be released to me again or sent to an auction house. Nevertheless,

I had bigger worries at that moment. I'd never before spent even an instant in a jail, not to mention a full-fledged correctional facility.

After waiting for the flatbed tow truck to show up to transport the motorcycle, the ranger put me into the back seat of his SUV. Sitting there, looking forward, I noticed there was a single blue light on his dashboard to be used when in pursuits. I never saw it flashing. While I'd been kneeling on the road, I'd heard a sheriff ask the arresting officer why his SUV's exterior wasn't properly outfitted with a light bar and crash bars and such. He responded that the vehicle was new and they hadn't finished installing a number of things.

During the 45-minute drive to the facility, the pain of the handcuffs became unbearable. The arresting officer had taken off the other ranger's cuffs, replacing them with his. My hands were facing each other back-to-back behind me, which is what was making the cuffs so painful. I mentioned this to him, and he responded that is how rangers purposely put handcuffs on people because it makes it more difficult to escape.

As the drive continued, the officer asked me if I was with those other motorcyclists. I thought that was an interesting question and told him I wasn't, which was 86% true. I wondered why that might matter to him.

Reviewing the events of that afternoon, I realized that both cars I had come up behind had stopped in the middle of the road because their drivers must have heard a siren or saw a flashing light in their mirrors. I heard no siren and saw no flashing lights. Motorcycle mirrors aren't great. I have since taught myself that when drivers act strangely I shouldn't assume they have simply become temporarily insane. It's much better to look for a logical reason why they're doing something that seems so senseless and unpredictable.

Upon finally reaching the correctional facility, we pulled up to two giant metal swinging doors about 18 feet tall and wide enough for a tractor trailer to pass through. The ranger radioed someone and a few moments later the doors slowly swung open. We drove into a narrow, roofed alley surrounded by windowless walls and stopped. I turned my head to watch the giant doors close behind us, leaving behind a life I knew. I felt as though I had just been swallowed by a heartless fate beyond my control.

For now, I'll only say that I am not a convicted felon. If this book proves to be of interest to readers, I will release a second book of collected columns and untold tales of bad behavior that will feature the conclusion of this adventure.

Peter Jones has "worked" as a motojournalist for more than 20 years. His first full-time editorial position was at Petersen Publishing's Sport Rider Magazine. Following that, Jones was an editor at 2wf.com and American Roadracing Magazine. He was also the founding editor of the urban performance magazine Motorcycle Street & Strip. Jones' freelance contributions have appeared in Baggers Magazine, Cycle News, Cycle World, Motorcycle Cruiser, Motorcycle Consumer News, Motorcyclist, Rider, Road Rider, RoadRUNNER, and numerous online publications.

Prior to becoming a motojournalist, Jones cofounded Team Swine Dudes with Tim Taylor. The team competed in the WERA National Endurance Series from 1990 to 1995. As Team Swine Dudes, and later as Team Pearls Suzuki, the team won three class championships and finished second overall twice. Team Pearls Suzuki also competed in the AMA Pro Racing Series in 1996 with rider Frank Wilson finishing 12th in the Daytona 200 and as the first privateer. The field included nearly 20 factory entries from the AMA, WorldSBK, and British and Japanese Superbike Series.

During his years as a motorcycle journalist, Jones has crashed motorcycles on racetracks, set a land speed record with the ECTA at 202.247 mph, dropped a $100,000 motorcycle while doing a U-turn, broken bones, injured other riders, traveled to the distant sides of oceans, and broken bread with racers who are far, far more talented on motorcycles.

In 2017, an oncoming pickup truck pulled into Jones' lane, planning on making a left turn across his path. Jones and the truck collided head-on. As a result, Jones got a full appreciation of ABS and a new motorcycle. Little else was gained from the incident.

Made in the USA
Middletown, DE
11 June 2021